THE FATHER-INFANT RELATIONSHIP

Statue of mother, father, and child by Gustav Vigeland. Vigelandsparken, Oslo.

THE FATHER-INFANT RELATIONSHIP

Observational Studies in the Family Setting

Edited by
Frank A. Pedersen

PRAEGER

PRAEGER SPECIAL STUDIES • PRAEGER SCIENTIFIC

Library of Congress Cataloging in Publication Data

Main entry under title:

The Father-infant relationship.

    Bibliography: p.
    1. Infants. 2. Father and child. I. Pedersen,
Frank A.
HQ774.F37   301.42'7   79-20514
ISBN 0-03-049506-7

Published in 1980 by Praeger Publishers
CBS Educational and Professional Publishing
A Division of CBS, Inc.
521 Fifth Avenue, New York, New York 10017 U.S.A.

123456789 145 98765432

Printed in the United States of America

PREFACE

Among the romantic metaphors to which scientific efforts are likened, images of a quest, a voyage of discovery, or an expedition to scale a previously unclimbed mountain peak frequently occur. A less evocative but perhaps more apt comparison of scientific effort in developmental psychology is to a bicycle race, in particular, a road race. In both activities the "professionals" begin their endeavors with years of intensive training and experience behind them, hoping to effect a favorable outcome through a combination of personal prowess, keen judgment, and refined technology. Scientific effort and a bicycle race initially proceed at a rather conservative pace: the participants act as a single group; responsibility for the lead is shared among many; and few risks are taken. In psychology, this means sticking to such well-proved topics as mother-infant interaction, cognitive development, and attachment behavior.

To continue the metaphor, in a bicycle race, somewhere along the route, a single person or a small group of individuals characteristically attempts to establish a "break." This means a few quickly accelerate the pace, hoping to establish a significant lead on the following "pack." By working together, the members of the break transform the entire race. A rider who "misses the break" cannot even hope for victory. Often the following pack will attempt to organize itself in an effort to make contact with the break. Sometimes a few will move ahead to join the break; sometimes the pack swallows up the break, only to have the process repeat itself further along in the race. Whatever the final outcome, at the time that a break occurs, the character of the overall race is changed radically by the combined efforts of a few.

In an expansive reverie, I think of the contributors to this volume as members of a break who have set a new pace for the field to follow. Their research work has begun to have an impact upon developmental psychology and notions of infants' early experiences. The purpose of this book, therefore, is to capture these ideas in their present state in the ongoing process of understanding human development.

The original basis for this collection of studies was a thought-provoking symposium held at the meetings of the Society for Research in Child Development in New Orleans in 1977. The series of papers was an uncommonly coherent collection, addressing a single topic: early experience in the nuclear family with a special focus on the father's role. Three of the final chapters (Lamb, Chapter 2; Parke and Sawin, Chapter 3; Clarke-Stewart, Chapter 6) are elaborations of the original symposium presentations. Two chapters present new data (Belsky, Chapter 5; Pedersen, Anderson, and Cain, Chapter 4), findings that were not available in 1977 but are central to the issues the book addresses. An introductory chapter presents a conceptual and methodological perspective for examining the problem, and there is a concluding, integrative chapter that pulls together the core findings from each investigation. Thus, this volume includes considerably more information than that communicated in the original symposium. Our hope is to achieve a combined impact that is more integrated and compelling than would be possible if the papers were published as separate journal reports, subject to the constraints imposed by brevity.

I am especially grateful to each of the authors who contributed to the volume. An editor's work can have special elements of pleasure when it is done with colleagues who combine a high level of professional competence, dedication to the task, and a sense of humor that keeps all in perspective. Appreciation is expressed to Leon J. Yarrow, my mentor in developmental psychology and English teacher of long-standing, for his encouragement and support of my work at the Child and Family Research Branch, National Institute of Child Health and Human Development. Barbara Anderson and Richard Cain, my coauthors for Chapter 4 and colleagues in research endeavors, also deserve recognition that goes beyond their contribution to this book. Appreciation is expressed to Martha Zaslow, who helped in many ways, not the least of which was her assumption of responsibility for the direction of my research program during the period I was at the University of Aarhus, Denmark. Terence Moore's comments on early versions of some of the chapters were helpful. I acknowledge support from the Institute of Psychology, University of Aarhus where the manuscript was completed. Finally, a special note of appreciation is given to Vibeke Schou, who, working in a language different from her native Danish, did an excellent job of preparing the final copy of the manuscript.

CONTENTS

LIST OF TABLES AND FIGURES

1

RESEARCH ISSUES RELATED TO FATHERS AND INFANTS

Frank A. Pedersen

The proposition addressed in this volume is that the father, as well as the mother, is a significant figure in the infant's social environment. This idea goes beyond traditional theory and research on early experience, which have focused almost exclusively on the mother-infant relationship. Studies of early influences on development have treated the mother as if she comprised the infant's entire social milieu, and theory has been concerned with mother and infant as if theirs was the only relationship infants formed.

More than a decade ago, there were convincing research findings that infants formed multiple attachments early in life (Schaffer and Emerson 1964), often with the father in addition to the mother. Yet, only recently have investigators taken these findings seriously with efforts to describe both the distinctive and similar aspects of the father-infant and mother-infant relationships. Research attention has focused only of late on the consequences of variation in the father-infant relationship for subsequent development. But if this new scientific regard for fathers is concentrated solely upon father and infant without concurrent attention to the larger family constellation of which it is a part, then it will be as shortsighted as the past emphasis upon mother and infant alone. The purpose of this volume is to address, by means of observational studies, the father's contributions to the infant's experiences in the nuclear family. Our thesis is that the infant's interaction involving the father can be understood fruitfully only in the context of relationships with other family members as well.

This chapter will consider why researchers guided by traditional theory have overlooked the father-infant relationship and why the importance of this relationship within the family is now being recognized and examined. Alternative research strategies will be evaluated briefly, and basic questions will be posed, which the chapters to follow will address.

1

CONCEPTUAL BARRIERS TO RESEARCH
ON THE FATHER-INFANT RELATIONSHIP

Both the selection of a research problem regarding the nature of early experience and the establishment of a design and methodology for evaluating hypotheses are processes guided by psychological theory. A theory may be explicit and well articulated, or it may be vague, diffuse, and little more than a set of sensitizing concepts. As surely as scientific efforts are guided by some conceptual framework, however explicit or implicit it may be, these conceptual guides also exert an enormous influence on defining the important research questions of the day. Further, it appears certain that theories of human experience are especially prone to the influence of dominant cultural values in any given historical period (Winthrop 1961). The test of the enduring value of a theory of human experience is its capacity to embrace new information as it arises—to validate new predictions in the face of changing social or cultural circumstances in the world. To put it more concretely, theory is a road map, a schematic guideline to the terrain. While representing some information quite well, at the same time it may fail to include other kinds of information, which becomes apparent to those who make forays into the territory it is intended to chart. Indeed, prevailing theory—just as antiquated road maps—can become totally misleading.

Until quite recently there have been many conceptual barriers that have interfered with considering the father as a significant figure in the infant's social milieu. Among these are the following: (1) stereotypic conceptions of family roles, (2) developmental theories that focus exclusively upon maternal influences, (3) chasms between theories regarding the marital relationship and the parent-infant relationship, and (4) concepts of the infant that fail to appreciate early competences and adaptive capacities that make possible interaction in a more complex environment than that encompassed solely by the mother. As will be seen, these conceptual barriers arise from several sources and, operating in concert, constitute an extraordinarily restrictive influence on thinking about the infant's environment.

Stereotypic Conceptions of Family Roles

Every culture has its own definition or set of expectations regarding the nature of the family: what constitutes a family; how family members are differentiated from each other on the basis of gender, age, or kinship; and what comprises appropriate repertoires of behavior for members of these groups. These expectations, which range from highly specific to rather broad prescriptions, exist at both an internalized, personal level and at a more public level, as articulated by members of the culture who are accorded authority to say what a family "ought" to be.

In recent years in the United States there has been a shift toward acceptance of alternative formulations of family roles. One now sees latitude for variation or experimentation in alternative expressions of what constitutes a family and for variation in behaviors that previously have been in the domain of one parent or the other. But these changes are recent developments. Deeply ingrained "traditional" conceptions of the family, which have been advanced at both the scholarly and popular levels, have not been swept aside. The stereotypic, traditional conception of the family is one factor that has acted to minimize appreciation of the nurturing capacities of fathers in relation to infants.

A widely held view* is that the industrial revolution and subsequent urbanization led to extreme differentiation in parental roles and a sharp division between the home and places of employment (Aries 1962; Oakley 1976). The traditional nuclear family, as it evolved in Western industrialized societies, thus came to prescribe the primacy of the economic-provider role for the husband/father and the child care and "homemaker" role for the wife/mother. This differentiation is embraced most explicitly in Parson's role theory (Parsons and Bales 1955). Parsons characterizes the male role as primarily "instrumental" in nature, oriented to the external world and responsible for establishing the social and economic position of the family in society. The female role is oriented to the home and is primarily "expressive" in nature. The wife/mother is responsible for the emotional and affective climate of the home, the nurturance of the young, and the majority of the domestic caretaking activities. The father's role in regard to children is expected to be important after the infancy period, when the child is more mature and capable of interaction with the larger social world. At this stage of development, the father becomes important especially to male children as a model for autonomy, achievement, and independence.

Sociologists have gathered evidence to disprove the validity of this portrayal of extreme role differentiation and complementarity between men and women in the family (Bernard 1975; Oakley 1976). Its constraining elements have been noted, particularly the depreciation of women: relegating them to the home and child care responsibilities, which society judges to have no economic value; disregarding their capacities and performance in work settings outside the home; and ascribing pejorative personality attributes to them, which focus on emotionality, dependency, and "mindless" traits. To a lesser degree, critics of stereotyped traditionalism have noted that men also are

---

*A dissenting interpretation of the causal influence of industrialization on family role differentiation has been offered by Goode (1970).

oppressed by role expectations that require pursuing uninterrupted work commitments and sanction against emotional expressiveness, nurturant tendencies, and dependency needs (Balswick and Peck 1971).

In spite of this criticism, Rapoport (1978) has called attention to the pervasiveness of stereotyping in the choice of research topics regarding marriage and the family. She maintains that studies often have attempted to corroborate these notions of family roles and that departures from modal normative formulations tend to be evaluated as deviant and potentially "pathological." Moreover, the male role of wage earner is so taken for granted in studies of the family that interest in the father often has been restricted solely to his level of educational and occupational attainments. Until quite recently there have been few research investigations of the nurturing role of fathers, their behavior when interacting with young infants, and the degree of emotional investment that parenting represents. In this volume the endeavor is made to break away from the conception that defines the father's contribution to the family so narrowly in terms of instrumentality in order to understand other aspects of his relationship with both infant and mother.

Developmental Theories Which Focus Exclusively Upon the Monther-Infant Relationship

Theories of the infant's early experiences are primarily oriented to the mother alone. The origin of this conceptual perspective undoubtedly predates Freud and must be deeply influenced by the universal biological fact that the mother gives birth to the young and, in most cultures, nurses and provides primary care for the infant for an extended period of time. Technology has only slightly modified these facts by the availability of nursing bottles and formulas. But it was Freud who focused attention upon the consequences of qualitative variation in the relationship between mother and infant, in this way hypothesizing the overarching primacy of the mother-infant dyad.

Freudian theory, and its more ego-oriented derivatives, gave special emphasis to the feeding experience and postulated that subsequent psychological development rested upon the successful negotiation of this stage. The father's role was conceived as largely peripheral until the oedipal period (age three to five years).* In studies of the early mother-infant relationship, many investigations were conducted of both specific feeding practices and the psychological climate surrounding feeding as well as other aspects of child care, attempting

---

*Recent writing in psychoanalytic theory (Burlingham 1973; Forrest 1967; Abelin 1971, 1975) deals with the father's positive contribution to development at earlier years.

to find sequelae in later personality or behavioral traits. While adherents to psychoanalytic theory may protest that attempts to define psychoanalytic concepts were excessively literal, the results from the majority of these studies were not strongly supportive of the theory. Orlansky (1949) found meager empirical support in his review of over 100 investigations of psychoanalytical hypotheses regarding infant care practices. So strong was the influence of Freudian theory, however, that he nevertheless concluded that further investigations should be undertaken. Another bleak evaluation was make by Caldwell (1964), which appears to mark a turn toward other theoretical perspectives in developmental psychology.

Two subsequent theoretical developments reaffirmed the centrality of the mother-infant relationship but cast the nature of early experience in a different light. The first was a shift away from drive-reduction concepts of reinforcement. The drive-reductionist position, basically a learning theory reinterpretation of psychoanalytic principals, held that the mother acquired positive secondary reinforcement value because of her association with drive-reducing provision of food and comfort. From these experiences the mother became a "generalized secondary reinforcer," and the infant established a relationship of special intensity with her. Among the most critical evidence challenging this position was Harlow's (1958) classic paper, evocatively titled "The Nature of Love." Harlow demonstrated that for rhesus monkeys tactile contact was a stimulus much preferred to experiences associated with the source of hunger reduction. Further evidence was offered from other investigators that much behavior appears to be stimulation seeking (Hebb 1949; Hunt 1961; White 1959) and can in no way be explained by drive-reduction concepts. Moreover, studies of institutional environments called attention to the fact that variation in amount and quality of sensory stimulation may affect development (Casler 1968).

The second major development was the emergence of attachment theory, especially the contributions of Bowlby (1951, 1969). Bowlby was greatly concerned with the effects of separation from parents and the influence of institutional environments on children's development, a phenomenon called "maternal deprivation."* In order to understand the effects of separation from mothers by infants, Bowlby thought it desirable first to study the developmental course of social attachments. His theoretical position drew from the psychoanalytic theory of object relations, ethological theory, and control systems theory.

-----

*Virtually all maternally deprived children in institutions were equally paternally deprived, but so little was thought of the paternal relationship that barely any mention was made of it.

Bowlby emphasized the crucial importance of mothering in the infancy period, and this has sometimes been interpreted to imply that any separation experience is potentially harmful. Of greater consequence to the issues addressed later in this volume, one of his special contributions was to recognize that it is the infant's various behaviors—tracking the mother visually and exhibiting signaling behaviors such as crying, smiling, and vocalizing and approach behaviors such as seeking, clinging, and sucking—that are important elicitors of nurturance and maintain proximity between mother and infant. Bowlby also interpreted these behaviors in terms of evolutionary principals, proposing that survival of the species is enhanced by the mother-infant attachment relationship. Bowlby's theoretical ideas stimulated much empirical research on the mother-infant relationship, both in controlled laboratory settings and the natural environment (Ainsworth 1969).

While these theoretical developments occurred in the context of understanding interaction beween mother and infant, they contained bases for increasing the credibility of the idea that infants form significant relationships with the father as well as the mother. Stimulation theory, as opposed to drive-reduction concepts of reinforcement, accords some import to the common observation that many fathers frequently become engaged with infants in bouts of arousing and activating social interactions. Attachment theory, recognizing the potency of the infant's behavior in eliciting nurturant responses, can accommodate the fact that people other than the biological mother also may respond to such cues. Indeed, evolutionary theory posits a survival advantage if a species with a long period of helplessness can be nurtured by more than a single agent (Freedman 1974; Hess 1970). Finally, attachment theory has encouraged descriptive research in the natural life setting, which in turn has yielded the first empirical findings that infants form multiple attachment relationships (Schaeffer and Emerson l964; Ainsworth 1963). The point remains, however, that the mainstream of theoretical development regarding early experience has focused on the mother-infant relationship.

Chasms Between Theories Regarding the Marital Relationship and the Parent-Child Relationship

Research and theory regarding the marital relationship, while appropriately according interest in both marital partners, have not directed attention to understanding interaction between father and infant. Studies of the male adult as husband have rarely been extended to understanding his contribution to parental experience. In part, this omission appears to be the result of rigid disciplinary prerogatives that have become established between sociology and psychology. Reubin Hill (1966) observed that psychologists have shown a curious disdain for studying the family as a social unit. In his review and synthesis of decades of research on marriage and the family, he commented:

> The psychologist, utilizing all of the frames of reference available to his discipline, finds himself focusing almost exclusively on the developing and responding child. His framework rarely permits him to include in his vision the many other positions, and the family as a group to be studied in its own right is absent from all the psychological frames of reference we have analysed to date. [Hill 1966]

A similar observation was made by Aldous (1977), who noted that the scoiologist's primary concern with the interaction has been in the marital relationship, while the parent-child relationship is of secondary importance. The psychologist's set of priorities in family relationships has been of the reverse order. This now appears to be an "unexpressed working relationship" between the disciplines, which may stand in the way of a more integrative understanding of experience in the family.

One consequence of this disciplinary cleavage is that certain research questions have received little attention—for example, the nature of psychological linkages between the marital and mother-child or father-child relationships. Stated in more general terms, these are questions of how the interactions between two people are affected by a third person. Influences of this nature have been called "second-order" effects by Bronfenbrenner (1974a) or "indirect" effects by Lewis and Weinraub (1976). At the simplest level, the mere physical presence of another may affect interaction between two people. Psychologically more meaningful formulations of the problem address the relationship or interaction between two people as a factor affecting each's behavior with another. The question that has received the greatest attention is whether the father, by providing emotional support to the mother, affects mother-infant interaction (Feiring and Taylor 1978; Pedersen 1975; Price 1977). Since this is but one of a very complex array of possible influences that may be formulated for a family of only three people, it is not surprising that no investigation has traced these influences comprehensively. Broader appreciation of the father's multiple roles in the family will be achieved by moving beyond the "fiction of convenience" that dyadic relationships exist in psychological isolation from other family members.

Difficulty in pursuing integrative research linking the marital and parent-infant relationships also may stem from the two areas being investigated with different methodologies. Research on the marital relationship has been based to a very great extent upon self-report procedures, both interviews and questionnaires. To a lesser extent, observational techniques have been employed, but results rarely show much convergence between approaches (Olsen 1969). Research on the parent-child relationship, although often based on parental reports years ago, now relies heavily on direct observational methods. Findings also show that observational and self-report techniques produce different results

(Lytton 1974; Yarrow, Campbell, and Burton 1968). Chapter 4 illustrates that a single observational strategy may be applied fruitfully to interaction among all family members in the infancy period. Perhaps advances in achieving an integrative understanding of the family depend, in part, upon utilizing a consistent methodological approach to its different component relationships.

Infant Competencies

There has been a dramatic change attributed to psychological research in the understanding of infancy. Previous theories conceived of the infant as a passive organism for whom the environment represented "booming, buzzing confusion." This position has been superseded by detailed information of early sensory and adaptational capacities that equip the infant to enter into a remarkably complex reciprocal relationship with a caregiver. Perhaps another important reason why fathers have been ignored in the infancy period is that, until recently, infants were not conceived of as capable of making the complex discriminations and responses necessary to enter into multiple relationships.

Mother-infant and father-infant interactions, particularly when they occur in close proximity to each other, provide the basis for a wide range of sensory discriminations, which experimental evidence suggests are within the young infant's capacities. Such discriminations include differences in: the visual configurations of the mother's and father's faces; frequency range, intensity, and modulation of their voices; olfactory perception; vigor and tempo of physical movements involving the baby's body; and behavior that is responsive to the infant's needs and signals. It is plausible that many of these discriminations occur in many interaction situations. For example, it is not unusual to observe the young infant apparently make visual comparisons between two people at the time when the baby is being transferred from one person to another. At the very least, such opportunities to make perceptual discriminations are likely to provide the basis for more complex later discriminatory learning.

The infant's early discriminative competencies have traditionally been thought of as providing the basis for the development of a focused relationship with the mother; the infant learns to distinguish the mother from "others." It is also possible that these discriminative and adaptational capacities provide the basis for subsequent differential relationships. Using highly refined observational technology and microanalysis of interaction sequences, Yogman (1977) has suggested that the three-to-five-month-old infant has differential expectations during face-to-face interactions with its mother and father and that the infant can regulate its own behavior to maintain synchrony with either parent. In an early investigation based on maternal report (Pedersen and Robson 1969), there is evidence that nine-month-old infants show differential expectancy patterns for fathers and mothers. About three-fouths of a sample of middle-class infants were reported to show " greeting behaviors" to their fathers upon reunions that followed time out of the home associated with work. These greetings consisted of smiles, vocalizations, bursts of excitement, and efforts to approach the fathers. The most obvious interpretation was that pleasurable interactions were anticipated from the fathers at that time. The expectations appeared differential because few mothers reported similar glee to their own reunions, perhaps because few had such predictable absences. Infant excitement with the mother was more typically associated with a particular caretaking activity, such a a bath or a familiar social game.

Postulating that the infant has the capacity to enter into early multiple relationships is quite different from proposing that there is some interchangeability among people who can enter into an intense relationship with the infant on an individual basis. The later view is exemplified in Schaffer's recent volume titled, *Mothering* (1977). After describing the essential components of the mother-infant relationship, Schaffer discussed relationships between infant and people other than the biological mother. He accepted interchangeability among people who may assume the mothering role and asserted that the mother ♣can be any person of either sex." Schaffer said, indeed, that the father can be the mother "if that is the role that he and his wife choose it to be." As a departure from Shaffer's idea, a thorough appreciation of the infant's competencies suggests that more than one such intense relationship is possible.

It is proposed here that several conceptual barriers arising from different scientific disciplines may have interfered with giving appropriate consideration to the relationship between father and infant. But scientific theory is never entirely static; new developments, even those advanced primarily to understand mother-infant interaction, have added credibility to the proposition that the infant and both parents are able to form meaningful relationships with each other.

MARKERS OF CHANGE IN PATERNAL BEHAVIOR

There are indications that, compared to earlier historical periods, middle-class men in the United States are likely to be more highly involved with infants in both caregiving and playful activities. A number of recent events are both markers of this secular trend and influences toward further change. Among the areas where changes have occured are the following: (1) childbirth practices, (2) patterns of participation in the work force outside the home, and (3) a variety of developments that, collectively, represent changing ideological perspectives regarding sex roles. These changes are unlikely to have effected a total revolution in paternal behavior, but it is important to monitor secular trends that, over the longer term, influence consensual notions of parenting. As in all cultural change, various subgroups are likely to be affected at different and perhaps unpredictable rates. The important point is that it is imperative for theoretical models of experience in the family to reflect accurately current social realities. A monotropic theory of the infant's social world may seriously misrepresent the nature of early experience.

Childbirth Practices

One of the most controversial specialties of U.S. medicine is obstetrics, and explicating detailed historical trends in childbirth practices falls beyond the scope of this chapter. Briefly, a major development has occurred that may be described grossly as a reaction against viewing childbirth as a disease, with its attendant massive medical interventions. The emphasis is now upon understanding and experiencing childbirth as an event occurring "naturally" in the course of the life cycle. Several important publications have had a pivotal influence on preparation for childbirth and on the actual events that transpire when childbirth occurs. Among these are *Childbirth without Fear* (Dick-Read 1959), *Painless Childbirth* (Lamaze 1970), and *Husband-Coached Childbirth* (Bradley 1965).

In broad outline, the natural childbirth movement* provides information and preparatory experiences regarding the nature of pregnenacy and delivery to both mother and father. By overcoming anxiety and fear, the goal is to make childbirth possible with minimal medical intervention, especially medications that may be potentially harmful to the newborn infant. An important feature is that effort is made to restore significant social relationships to childbirth, a practice more common in primitive and less technologically dominated societies than in the modern hospital environment. Labor and delivery occur in the presence of a trained and emotionally supportive partner, often the husband who participated with the wife in the preparatory program. According to one investigation, not only does the mother characteristically feel the importance of their being together, but most men who participate in labor and delivery speak positively about their experiences (Fine 1976). Some advocates of participative childbirth stress that the sense of family is strongly established during the birth process and that fathers especially benefit in contrast to being isolated from childbirth in a traditional "waiting room" (Tanzer and Block 1972; Kitzinger1972).

---

*Perhaps a more suitable term is *participative childbirth* because a key element of the movement emphasizes the active involvement of both mother and father in the birth process.

Carefully controlled research investigations that differentiate the effect of self-selection, the preparation program, and the birth experience itself apparently have not been done. But it is clear that the natural childbirth movement has changed birth experiences dramatically. In one investigation that attempted to evaluate the effect of Lamaze training and the father's presence during delivery, virtually all fathers in the "control" group were discovered to have also attended the delivery of their infants (Wente and Crockenberg 1976). It is at least a reasonable hypothesis that the remarkably intense emotional experience of childbirth sensitizes the father to being an active and involved parent. The enduring effects of this experience would, of course, be influenced by subsequent interactions with wife and baby.

Another recent change in medical practices, which may be seen as a development of the participative childbirth movement, concerns the parents' experiences with the baby in the immediate postpartum period. Largely through the influence of pediatriacians Marshall Klaus and John Kennell, efforts have been made to minimize the separation between mother and infant that often occurs in hospital deliveries. Arguing initially from ethiological data on various animal species, Klaus and Kennell (1976) proposed that the earliest interaction between mother and infant—within minutes of the bith—serves to establish the bond of the mother to the infant and that there is a biological basis for early and continuing contact with the mother. There is thought to be a sensitive period immediately after childbirth, and the infant acts as a stimulus for the mother to elicit nurturant behavior. Disruption of the opportunities for immediate contact, even that associated with traditional hospital routines, possibly interfers with the bonding and subsequent development of an attachment relationship. Extreme separation experience, such as that experienced with a premature delivery, is considered a threat to the mother-infant bond and may increase the likelihood of problems in the later development of the child.

Klaus and Kennell (1976) have presented findings from several investigations that argue that there are lasting effects of early contact on subsequent mother-infant interaction. Assuming the validity of these findings, there remains the interesting question of whether psychological factors explain the findings. If the effects of early contact between mother and infant are largely due to psychological influences (that is, are not unique to the mother's biological state), then it seems likely that the behavior of fathers may be affected by early contact with the baby. The opportunity to hold and touch the newborn infant may affect father-infant bonding, promoting a closer relationship than characteristically occurs when the father is separated from the birth experience. Even though the psychological aspects of childbirth are not fully understood for either father or mother, it is clear that the birth experience and both parents' opportunities for contact with the newborn infant have radically changed in the past decade. There is the possibility that, especially for families who have sought out such experiences, participative childbirth promotes a more intense relationship between parent and offspring as well between parents.

Changes in Work Force Participation Outside the Home

One of the most clearly documented secular trends bearing on family roles is the dramatic increase in rates of participation of women in the work force outside the home. Of women in the United States in two-parent families with school-age children, the proportion who are employed outside the home exceeded 50 percent in 1972 (Hoffman 1977). This figure has been steadily increasing in spite of historically high unemployment rates, and similar trends are evident in other idustrialized nations (Cook 1978). Moreover, the rate of increase in work force participation appears greatest for women with very young children. In the period in which employment rates doubled for mothers with school-age children, there was a threefold increase for mothers with pre-school-age children. In 1976 fully one-third of U.S. mothers with children under age three years were employed, an increase of seven precentage points in only five years (U.S. Department of Labor 1977).

There are important implications of this trend for considering the father-infant relationship. First, research data indicate that in families where the mother works outside the home the father is more likely to show greater involvement in child care compared to families in which the mother is not employed outside the home. Although the validity of this generalization has been disputed (Cook 1978), the evidence appears clear in more carefully controlled investigations. An unpublished doctoral thesis by Young (1975) reports that, in small but carefully matched samples of one-year-old infants, fathers in families where the mother works outside the home spent more time in close proximity to the infant and performed more caretaking activities than did the fathers in families where the mother did not work outside the home. Other studies that control for family size also show similar findings (Hoffman1977).

It is possible that the more recent trend toward maternal employment with very young children will ultimately have an even stronger influence on paternal behavior. In the past, the mother more characteristically returned to the work force as the youngest child reached school age; this transition occurred after the family had experienced several years in which its patterns of maternal specialization in child care had had an opportunity to become solidified. The entry of the mother into the work force at that point may have been accompanied by relatively little change in the father's established pattern in regard to child care and household participation. When the mother of a very young child works outside the home, paternal sharing in child care is likely to be encouraged from the outset.

Another implication of the increase in maternal employment is that mothers and fathers may eventually spend more similar time periods with their children, changing great disparities that now exist. When the father is the wage earner and the mother provides the primary child care, the mother often experiences long periods of time on a purely one-to-one basis with the baby to the point where she may feel deprived of adult interaction. This role organization tends to set a natural limit on how much time the father spends on a strictly one-to-one basis with the baby, a factor that may lead to a rather narrow repertoire in his ways of relating to the infant. When both parents participate outside the home as wage earners, they also have more similar opportunities for interacting and providing care for the child. Of course, individual attitudes, values, and ideologies may influence how time with the baby is used. Interestingly, obervational studies comparing the quality of parent-infant interaction for both mother and father when the family has alternative role organization have not yet been reported. It is likely that secular changes in work force participation will influence both the father's and mother's behavior in the infancy period, but careful documentation of these effects remains to be done.

Changes in Conceptions of Sex Roles

In addition to changes in childbirth experiences and patterns of work force participation, both of which have implications for the paternal role, a broader attitudinal or ideological shift is evident that is a concomitant of such change and a force in its own right. Already alluded to in discussion of previous topics, a number of developments have occurred that, collectively, point toward acceptance of less-differentiated gender roles for men and women. One of the principal influences behind this development is the women's rights movement, although the effects of technological, economic, and other societal changes are also relevant (Hoffman 1977; Goode 1970). The areas in which change toward greater equality between men and women are occuring are diverse and multifaceted: language forms referring to men and women, the portrayal of men's and women's roles in textbooks and the media, access to economic resources through work and advancement opportunities, and the reversal of legal precedents that discriminate against either men or women. There are many important implications of these developments for the father's role in the family, but the discussion will be limited to only two issues, one theoretical and one practical.

First, the conceptualization of sex roles in social science theory has been affected. The traditional theoretical approach to male and female role behavior has been in terms of a unidimensional, bipolar construct in which masculinity-femininity is roughly equated with the instrumental-expressive dimension (Parsons and Bales 1955). Similarly, Bakon (1966) conceptualized a dichotomy in which masculinity is associated with an "agentic" orientation, a concern with the individual manifested as self-protection, self-assertion, and self-expansion, and femininity is associated with a "communal" orientation, a sense of being at one with others and concerned for the relationship between oneself and others. As bipolar end points of a single dimension, these prespectives may be called "either-or" theories.

More recent theoretical formulations (Bakon 1966; Bem 1974; Block 1973; Heilbrun 1976; Spence and Helmreich 1978) may be described as "both-and" perspectives. The concept of *psychological androgyny* has been proposed to denote the integration in the same individual of both elements of the dichotomized dimensions discussed above. Psychological androgyny implies that it is possible for an individual to be both instrumental and expressive, both agentic and communal, depending upon behavioral requirements of particular situations. Moreover, in this model, personal maturity is associated with greater integration of these behavioral possibilities. Attention is now being directed to the socialization process—the internalization of values—in an effort to identify patterns of parental behavior that are associated with the development of psychological androgyny and personal maturity of the young (Block 1973; Spence and Helmreich 1978).

One practical implication for fathers of this shift in the conceptualization of the sex-role behavior is that latent tendencies for men to engage in nurturant behavior are being "legitimized." Whether behavioral changes precede attitudinal and ideological shifts, or the reverse, there are many indications that men have already embraced child care roles more readily than in the past. One statistic that confirms this trend is the increased proportion of men who have been granted legal custody of their children following divorce. Prior to 1960, very few fathers were awarded custody of their children, and then only in unusual circumstances. Between 1965 and 1972, a period of rapidly rising divorce rates, the rate of increase of single-parent families headed by the father was 15 percent greater than for families headed by the mother (Orthner, Brown, and Ferguson 1976). This trend appears related to widespread acceptance of no-fault divorce legislation, which often includes increased negotiation rights for custody of children on the part of the fathers. Recent legal precedents have been established that lend support to single-parent fatherhood as "an emerging life style."

While the trend for fathers to become the custodial parent following divorce does not speak directly to paternal behavior within the two-parent family, other changes are occurring that are more relevant. Instances of fathers providing primary care during infancy are prevalent enough to fall under the scrutiny of psychologists (Field 1978). Families are also experimenting with work-sharing patterns (Grønseth 1975), where each parent works part-time. In one of the first empirical studies of this family role organization, Grønseth reported that a major factor in the decision to attempt work sharing was the mutual wish of mother and father to share more equally in child care. Thus there appears to be a trend toward greater involvement of fathers with infants and young children, and a relaxation of the traditional sex-role prescriptions is likely to accelerate such changes.

While changes in paternal behavior have been emphasized, one must still regard many of these developments as but the leading edge of cultural shift. They are the lightly visible markers of changing family roles, but it does not appear that androgynous parenting is the current mode. Many more families embrace relatively traditional conceptions of their roles, and this is still a highly adaptive solution to meeting the needs of children and of the parents themselves in the prevailing economic structure.

In Fine's (1976) investigation of the transition to fatherhood, one important factor that contributed to an effective postpartum adjustment in men was developing some kind of coherent role rather than any particular role. He distinguished between men who adopted a "breadwinner" role, in which the fathers emphasized their financial responsibility with a distinct, mutually acceptable division of labor with their wives, and a "nontraditional" role, in which the fathers saw themselves as deeply involved in the daily care of their babies and divided most child care tasks with their wives. Either pattern seemed to work effectively, but men who experienced more difficulty after the birth were seen as having been less successful at working out mutually acceptable divisions of labor and roles with their wives in the postpartum weeks. That different adaptations are possible underscores the need for a firmer empirical base for understanding the full range of paternal behavior that affects infant's early experiences in the family.

RESEARCH STRATEGIES

Five research investigations will be presented in the chapters that follow. All studies focused on the infancy period (and some extended into toddlerhood) and all utilized observational methodologies in the home environment. The particular power of this strategy may be seen by contrasting it briefly with other methodological approaches. The assumption here is that the early stages in the scientific study of interpersonal relationships should be one of description. It will be apparent that for the particular questions being addressed an observational approach, to paraphrase the words of Churchill in describing democratic government, is a bad strategy, but it is better than all the rest.

Early investigations of father influences focused on older children and utilized an indirect approach: the comparison of children reared in father-absent families with children reared in father-present families. Biller (1974) has summarized this extensive literature. Herzog and Sudia (1973) provided valuable criticism of the technical and methodological limitations of many of these studies; they noted that differences between groups are due as likely to the larger social milieu accociated with father absence as they are due to the absence of the father per se. Father-absence investigations are not without importance, however. It is very likely that differences reported between father-absent and father-present groups of children were due to environmental influences. Bell (1968) has pointed out that correlational or group comparison research designs are often insensitive to the contribution of genetic or constitutional variables, which produce behavioral differences erroneously interpreted as due to environmental influences. It is unlikely that congenital factors could have influenced findings in studies of father absence.*

While results from the father-absence research paradigm implicate the father in some global way with the child's development, the more serious problem is that a simple emphasis on outcome (effects discernible in the child) does not illuminate psychological processes. A deficit-oriented approach does not direct attention to the father's actual behavior within the nuclear family. The father absence research strategy cannot contribute to knowledge of the father-child relationship any more than did research on the effects of understimulating institiutions enhance understanding of the child's experiences in the normal home environment (Pedersen 1976).

One of the first investigations that explicitly considered a variety of dimensions of father-infant interaction was based on interview data (Pedersen and Robson 1969), the mother's descriptions of the father's behavior with the child and the child's relationship with the father. In a more recent application of this methodology to investigate the father's role (Russell 1978), several precautions were noted to ensure that the data were valid. On balance, the interview appears useful and efficient for eliciting certain information, so long as the interview process itself does not evoke excessive anxiety or defensive maneuvers that greatly distort the information obtained. In a hypothetical investigation of the effects of different work roles outside the home on parent-child interaction, it would seem vastly more efficent to ask the parents about the nature of their work than to expand time in direct observation of work settings for the same information, The limitations of the interview must also be appreciated (1) the data obtained are the interviewee's verbal constructions of experience, filtered through lenses that may be biased in various directions and sometimes more indicative of the informant's cognitive processes than the events the interview purports to measure, and (2) the phenomena being investigated must be

---

*The reasoning behind this assertion is that the dependent variable in most investigations, such as the child's cognitive development or sex role identification, is unlikely to have been the principal reason for the father's absence from the family. This is particularly true when the dependent variable was appraised years after the father left the family. Thus, the causal direction of influence is relatively certain, even if the precise nature of influence is not.

apprehended in some way by the informant, and therefore subtle psychological events may simply not be available for study. More extensive treatment of the limitations of self-report and other attributional data are discussed by Donald Fisk in his recent book, *Strategies for Personality Research* (1978).

Data obtained by trained observers are also vulnerable to distortions (Rosenthal 1966). However, there are safeguards against bias in observational investigations—that is, through the use of several observers trained to utilize objective criteria and behavioral judgments relatively free from inference or evaluation. Further, by sensitizing the observers to the phenomena being studied, very subtle information may become available that is not retrievable by other methods.

For the research questions this volume addresses, the more moot issue concerns the usefulness of data obtained in the laboratory as compared to observations in the natural environment. Examples of several studies of the father-infant relationship utilizing laboratory paradigms were recently summarized by Kotelchuck (1976). Most findings were based on a variation of the Ainsworth Strange Situation (Ainsworth and Bell 1970), in which childrens's reactions were assessed to the departure from and reunion with either mother, father, or an unfamiliar adult. From the child's differential behavior in these episodes, inferences were made about the nature of the child's enduring relationship with either parent. Kotelchuck also mentioned studies that utilize both parental interviews and laboratory observations. For example, estimates of the father's characteristic caregiving practices were obtained by interview, while the laboratory was used to obtain criterion measures thought to be related, such as the child's behavior when left with a stranger (Kotelchuck 1972; Ross, Kagan, Zelazo, and Kotelchuck 1975).

The need to combine laboratory findings with some external measures, even those based on interviews, reveals the fundamental weakness of the laboratory approach alone. Interesting and reliable response differences still require some empirical ties with the more enduring environment. Too often, linkages are based on pure speculation; without empirical ties, the external validity of laboratory observation is unknown. The willingness of psychologists to accept experimental manipulation as inherently valid for a very wide range of questions, in addition to utilizing in many laboratory experiments situations that are unfamiliar, artificial, and short-lived, led Bronfenbrenner (1977) to characterize much of U.S. developmental psychology as "the science of the strange behavior of children in strange situations with strange adults for the briefest possible periods of time." To document his critique, Bronfenbrenner cited a survey of all studies in child development published between 1972 and 1974 in three prominent research journals. The experimental laboratory paradigm was employed in 76 percent of all investigations, while only 8 percent were observational studies in the natural environment.

The strongest arguments in favor of observational investigations in natural settings have been reasons of ecological validity. Cogent expression of this belief was stated by Willems (1977, p. 33):

> The ecologist recommends more dependence on direct, sustained
> naturalistic observations of human behavior and less on short-cut
> methods based on verbal expression and the handiest investigative
> location, which so often is the experimental laboratory. Question-
> naires, interviews, tests, and experiments all have one important
> characteristic in common: they require the subject to interrupt what
> he is doing in his natural context and perform a special task for
> the investigator.

Not all psychologists accept the simple premise that observation in the natural life setting automatically yields valid data. Of special concern has been the effect of the the presence of the observer on the phenomena being investigated. It seems likely that one influence of the observer on parents is to produce a heightened frequency of behaviors that the participants judge to be more socially desirable and inhibit behavior considered socially undesirable. Problems of this nature, the variable and largely unknown effect of the observer's presence, have not been studied extensively. What is known is largely confined to laboratory settings (Orne 1962; Graves and Glick 1978). Data by Belsky (1977), however, suggests that mothers' social desirability motives operate more strongly in laboratory than in home settings. An alternative solution, restricting research to unobtrusive measures (Webb, Campbell, Schwartz, and Sechrist 1966), would seem either to eliminate most of the phenomena of greatest theoretical interest or else raise important ethical issues because of using "invisible" technologies or involving families in research investigations without receiving their prior consent.

The safegards to the problem of the effects of the observer's presence employed by all of the investigations in this volume were the traditional ones: (1) in connection with securing informed consent from participants, all studies included meeting with parents before observations were made in order to reduce possible apprehension about the purpose of the investigation, and (2) the duration of the visit in the home setting was generally long enough so that the participants were able to feel comfortable with the observer and therefore not maintain a defensive posture in their behavior.

An interesting conceptualization of field research has been offered by Tunnell (1977). He identified three theoretically independent dimensions in methodologies, each of which injects a bit of the real world into psychological research. Research combining all three dimensions stands to become much richer, permit the most meaningful generalizations, and uncover the most important empirical relationships. The three dimensions of naturalness are: (1) natural behavior, which is not established primarily for the purpose of conducting research; (2) natural settings, a context not established for the sole or primary purpose of conducting research: and (3) natural treatments, events to which the subject is exposed that were not created solely by the researcher. To illustrate examples of each, natural behavior precludes interviews and questionnaires but includes the baby smiling or crying and parental play or caregiving; natural setting does not apply to the psychological laboratory but does include the home: natural treatments exclude a standardized approach to the baby by an unfamiliar adult displaying a fixed, unsmiling face but includes changes in group structure when one parent spontaneously leaves or enters the situation where the infant and other parent are interacting. All investigations in this volume draw their core data from sources combining two or three of these dimensions.

In summary, it is important to recognize that every methodology has its own unique combination of advantages and shortcomings. Methodologies ultimately must be evaluated in terms of their appropriateness for the research questions they are attempting to address.

THE RESEARCH QUESTIONS

The five investigations were developed in relative independence of each other. Each reflects the investigator's particular conceptual and methodological priorities, the scope of the problem that each chose to address, and the research resources that were available. By their diversity, many more questions were examined than if each study represented a narrow replication of the same problem. The special significance of the studies, however, lies in the fact that there are a number of core questions that were examined by more than one investigation. The value of replication is appreciated infrequently in behavioral science. But over the longer term, it appears that the ability to corroborate findings conributes at least as much to science as does the initial reporting of a new result. Therefore, the reader will find a mixture of both unique and repeated questions being addressed. Among the areas that are covered are the following:

Questions related to parental behavior

1. What are the differences as well as the similarities that mothers and fathers show in their behavior with infants and young children?
2. Are there variations in patterns of differences and similarities that are related to the age and sex of the child?
3. Do mother and father resemble each other more in certain activities, such as caregiving, than in other activities, such as social play?

Questions related to the behavior of infant or child

1.   What is the evidence regarding the infant's attachment relationship with either father or mother?
2.   Does age or sex of the child affect patterns of behavior directed toward either parent?

Questions about the spousal relationship and parent-infant interaction

1.   How is the quality of either parent's behavior toward the child altered when the other parent is also present in the same social setting?
2.   How does the husband-wife relationship affect either parent's behavior with the infant or child?

Questions about the child's developmental outcome

1.   Is there evidence that the mother and father have distinctive contributions to the child's cognitive or social development?
2.   How do the behaviors of mother or father interact to reinforce, modify, or dilute the other parent's impact upon the developing child?

These are the questions that the chapters to follow focus upon. The reader is cautioned that the answers may not fall out in neat little packages. The goal is to stimulate fresh thinking, a reconceptualization of early experience to include not only father-infant and mother-infant relationships but the relationship between the two parents and its impact on the infant.

2

THE DEVELOPMENT OF
PARENT-INFANT ATTACHMENTS IN
THE FIRST TWO YEARS OF LIFE

Michael E. Lamb

This chapter will present the results of partially overlapping longitudinal studies in which the development of mother-infant and father-infant attachments was traced between 7 and 24 months of age. The focus of this research was on social interaction—notably, those interactions between parent and infant that many believe to be the crucible of personality development. Studies of social development have become remarkably popular in recent years and the reason for this popularity is not difficult to identify. For the last 75 years (at least) all major theorists have stressed that early experiences have a disproportionately powerful impact on later development. In addition, the accessibility of infant subjects and the dramatic nature of the changes in personality and social competence during infancy have accelerated the popularity of infant research.

There are many theories to explain what happens during these months, each theory with its own depiction of the organism that is transformed (Ainsworth 1969; Gewirtz 1972). Yet amidst this vast diversity, there is one central assumption that unites all major theories—the presumption that the mother-infant relationship is, in Freud's (1948), words, "Unique, without parallel, established unalterably as the prototype of all later love relations."

The author's research was supported by two grants from the Ecology of Human Development Program of the Foundation for Child Development. Sheila Huddleston, Jamie Lamb, Judith McBride, Marilyn Stade, and Kinthi Sturtevant assisted in the collection and analysis of the data, and their invaluable help is gratefully acknowledged. M. Anne Easterbrooks and Susan Kay Bronson critically reviewed an earlier draft of this chapter.

The belief in the primacy and preeminence of the mother-infant relationship has become almost an article of faith to students of infant sociopersonality development, yet it is, to me, an unreasonable assumption. I am not troubled by the belief that mothers have a major impact on their infants' development. Indeed, all laws of learning and influence make that belief unavoidable. What is disturbing is the assumption, stated explicitly or implied unmistakably, that the mother-infant relationship is a uniquely and exclusively important determinant of infant personality development. Though most theorists acknowledge that subsidiary relationships may subsequently be formed—for example, with fathers and siblings—these are discussed almost parenthetically, as if they were of little significance for personality development. At best, other family members are seen as potentially useful, occasional substitute caretakers. Crudely speaking, they are seen as socializing agents who are qualitatively similar to, but quantitatively vastly inferior than, mothers.

From the time I began research on infant social development, this characterization has failed to satisfy me. It seems more reasonable to conceive of personality development in the context of a family system—a system into which the infant is integrated via relationships with mother, father, siblings, and so on. Finding this conceptualization unrepresented in the literature, the present study was undertaken to speak to this shortcoming. There are two major issues in this research. The first question was the only one to have been addressed previously: Are infants attached to both mothers and fathers, and if so, are mothers prefered to fathers as most theorists believe? The second question is: If infants are attached to both parents, does the nature of the mother-infant relationship differ from the nature of the father-infant relationship?

In addition to these two issues, data will be presented relevant to the question of parental preference, which were gathered in experimental rather than naturalistic contexts. These experiments yielded additional information concerning the effects of one parent's presence on the infant's interaction with its other parent, and these findings to will be discussed. The major findings, however, derive from two partially overlapping longitudinal studies undertaken in New Haven, Connecticut, between 1974 and early 1976.

THEORETICAL BACKGROUND

The dominant conceptual framework in the study of infant social development today is the ethologically oriented attachment theory of Bowlby (1969) and Ainsworth (1972, 1973). This study drew heavily on attachment theory for a number of reasons. It provides the most cohesive and useful theoretical structure currently available, it has been drawn upon extensively by previous researchers, and it proposes explicitly both that the mother-child relationship is the most important at any time and that the nature of the mother-child attachment determines the character of all subsequent relationships.

Relying primarily on evidence collected by ethologists and primatologists, Bowlby (1969) proposed that young infants are biologically predisposed to seek the proximity of adults who would, in humanity's "environment of evolutionary adaptedness" (that is, the environemnt is which *Homo sapiens* evolved, and for which, consequently, the species is biologically adapted), have protected defenseless human infants from potential predators. Until capable of independent locomotion, infants must rely on signals—such as vocalizing and crying—to get adults to approach and protect them. As they mature, however, infants gradually assume responsibility for active achievement and maintenance of proximity (compare Hinde and Spencer-Booth 1967; Hinde and Atkinson 1970).

During the first month or two of life, infants are indiscriminate in the display of these proximity-promoting behaviors (Ainsworth 1973; Bowlby 1969; Yarrow 1972). Gradually, however, infants come to direct these behaviors most often to the few people who participate in the most frequent and most consistent interaction, and these individuals become attachment figures. It is generally believed that infants are not attached to anyone until they attain six to eight months of age (compare Ainsworth 1969; Lamb 1978d). It is only at this age that infants have matured cognitively to such an extent that they have a primitive but adequate conception of the independent and permanent existence of other persons (compare Bell 1970; Decarie 1965). Furthermore, it is only at this age that infants begin to protest reliably when separated from their parents (Ainsworth 1962; Bowlby 1973). According to Bowlby, separation protest indicates that infants, who are no longer willing to accept substitutes, are attempting to recall the absent parents. The occurrence of protest in response to long-term separation (such as that occurring when a child is institutionalized) is seen as the most reliable way of assessing whether an infant is attached to a specific person. Clearly, however, this is an impractical operational definition for research on home-reared infants.

Recognizing this, Ainsworth (1964) presented a list of behaviors, known as attachment behaviors, which should be directed more often to attachment than nonattachment figures. The 13 behaviors were: crying, smiling, vocalizing, visual-motor orienting, crying upon separation, following, "scrambling" (that is, manually exploring the person), burying face in lap, exploring from a secure base, clinging, lifting arms in greeting, clapping hands in greeting, and approach through locomotion. The common characteristic of these behaviors is that they may serve either to bring the infants closer to adults or encourage the adults to approach or remain near the infants. Most researchers (including those whose primary commitment is clearly not to attachment theory) have drawn their measures from Ainsworth's list or from the more extensive list provided by Bowlby (1969). It must be remembered, though, that attachment behaviors are merely crude observable indexes that permit investigators to infer the existence of attachment bonds. Because they are relatively crude measures, it is important to take as many as possible in to account when conducting research. Many researchers have employed a limited number of measures, but this may limit both the validity of as well as the types of conclusions that can be drawn.

Attachment theorists see the attachment behavior system as one of four intermeshed systems mediating infant behavior—the others being the affiliative, exploratory, and fear/wariness systems (Bretherton and Ainsworth 1974; Lamb 1978d). They have recently stressed that many of Ainsworth's attachment behaviors may not be in the exclusive service of the attachment behavioral system. Many of these behaviors—such as smiling and vocalizing —are also essential for affiliative interaction with other friendly people. Consequently, in this study differentiation was made between these behaviors referred to as affiliative behaviors and those behaviors that are restricted largely to interaction with attachment figures, which are called attachment behaviors. The latter behaviors are those most closely related to physical contact and the desire for it.

Both theoretical (Bowlby 1969; Bretherton and Ainsworth1974) and empirical (Lamb 1976a; Tracy, Lamb, and Ainsworth 1976) considerations render important the distinction between attachment and affiliative behaviors. Although affiliative behaviors such as smiling and vocalizing may occur in the service of the attachment behavior system described by Bowlby, they also occur during interaction with friendly persons to whom the baby is not attached. Consequently, preferences in the display of such behaviors are difficult to interpret and tell the investigator little about the infant's enduring relationships or affective preferences. In the present report, it was assumed that the display of more affiliative behaviors to one person than to another indicated simply that the baby interacted more with the former person rather than that the person was a preferred attachment figure.

By contrast, the attachment behaviors should occur far more frequently in the course of interaction with attachment figures than with nonattachment figures. Preferences in the display of these behaviors would indicate that the infant was attached to one of the two comparison figures. In the present study, then, it was expected that infants would show no preference for either parent over the other in the display of attachment behaviors in the stress-free home environment, although they should evidence clear preferences for the two parents over an unfamiliar adult (the "visitor").

When studying infant preferences, many researchers attempt to determine whether attachment behaviors are directed most often to one person (for example, mother) rather than to another (for example, a "stranger"). The results obtained in evaluations of parental preferences have been remarkably inconsistent. Some studies have reported preferences for mothers over fathers in 10-to16-month-old babies (for example, Lewis and Weinraub 1974; Cohen and Campos 1974); others have reported no preference for either parent in

12-to24-month-olds (Feldman and Ingham 1975; Kotelchuck 1972; Lamb 1976c; Ross et al. 1975; Spelke et al. 1973; Willemsen et al. 1974). In all, then, there has been no satisfactory determination of parental preference—a rather significant deficiency if one considers the universal theoretical assumptions.

This study differed in several respects from its predecessors. First, it employed a longitudinal design, beginning with observations of the infants at seven and eight months of age—the age at which they should have been forming their first attachments. Further, most of the data were gathered in naturalistic home observations rather than in contrived laboratory contexts.

The study was designed to test several of Bowlby's assumptions. Attachment theory predicts that infants will become attached to their mothers sooner and that they will consistently prefer their mothers to their fathers. To confirm these predictions, we should find supportive evidence in the differential display of attachment behaviors. In addition, separation protest should follow departures by the mothers more reliably than by the fathers, and positive greetings should be more common following reunion with mothers than fathers.

METHODOLOGY

Subjects

The original subjects of the study were 10 male and 10 female infants recruited from the birth records of the Yale-New Haven Hospital. They came from white, traditional, relatively stable, lower- to upper-middle-class families. Only one of the families was affiliated with a university. In all families but one, the mother was the primary caretaker. In one family, the father (a graduate student) shared care for the baby with his wife, who worked part-time in order to supplement the family's income.

The babies were observed in their homes at times when both parents were present, when they were 7, 8, 12, and 13 months of age. Together, the first two visits shall be referred to as the early series, and the next visits as the later series. The visits each lasted between 1.5 and 2 hours. During the visits, the parents were asked to proceed with their normal routines as much as possible, although they were encouraged to remain in the same room as the child most of the time.

Since it seemed likely that the presence of an observer might cause both parents and infants to behave abnormally, the male observer was accompanied each time by the same female assistant, referred to as the visitor. Her purpose was to interact with parents and child as would any normal guest, alleviating their anxieties about being observed. When subsequently questioned, the parents generally stated that her presence had helped considerably and that family interaction had been quite typical.

All observations were made by the same observer who quietly dictated into a tape recorder a detailed narrative account of the infant's behavior and the contingent behaviors of the adults. While the observer was dictating, a timer automatically marked on the tape the passage of each 15-second time span. The tapes were subsequently transcribed and coded by one of three trained persons. In the observations and coding, the focus was on the display of affiliative and attachment behaviors, the reactions to separation and reunion, and the nature of play and physical contact interaction. Further details regarding the procedure as well as the behavioral definitions are available in two earlier publications (Lamb 1976b, 1977a).

The affiliative behaviors were smiling, vocalizing, looking, laughing, and proferring (that is, offering or sharing a toy). We were primarily interested in occasions where the baby directed one of these behaviors to a specific person; the affiliative measures were frequency counts, scored once each time the behavior occured.

The attachment behaviors recorded were proximity, approaches, touches, requests to be picked up, reaches, and fusses to an adult. Proximity was scored when the infant was within a three-foot radius of the person; an approach was scored when the infant moved from beyond to within this radius. Touching and proximity were duration measures, recorded once in every 15-second unit over which they extended. All other attachment behavior measures were frequency counts, scored once each time the behavior occurred.

Reliability

Observer reliability was computed by arranging for additional visits to the homes of several infants and observations of an additional group of babies. On these occasions, two observers independently dictated accounts of the infant's behavior. Coefficients were computed to express the proportion of the total number of occurrences of each behavior reported by one observer that were correctly reported by the other observer. Interobserver agreement in the recording of the attachment and affiliative behaviors was above .75 for all categories.

Intercoder agreement was likewise satisfactory. In addition to training sessions, approximately 10 percent of the transcripts were independently recoded by another coder, usually in circumstances such that neither person knew that reliability was being assessed. Reliability coefficients were usually above .90 and always above .85.

RESULTS AND DISCUSSION

The First Longitudinal Study

In considering the data on attachment and affiliative behavior, only those periods when both parents were in the room with the infant were utilized. With this constraint applied, the average duration of observation per infant was about 125 minutes in the early series and 160 minutes in the later series. All scores were converted to rates per minute to equalize the contributions made by each

TABLE 2.1

Patterns of Preferences in the Display of Attachment
and Affiliative Behaviors:
Seven- and-Eight-Month-Olds

Behavior	Mother versus Father	Father versus Visitor	Mother versus Visitor
Affiliative behaviors[a]	F > M[b]	—	—
Vocalizes	F > M[c]	F > V[d]	—
Smiles	F > M[d]	—	V > M[c]
Looks	F > M[f]	—	V > M[f]
Laughs	F > M[d]	—	—
Attachment behaviors[a]	F > M[d]	F > V[d]	M > V[c]
Approaches	—	—	—
Proximity[g]	—	—	—
Reaches	F > M[e]	F > V[e]	—
Touches	—	F > V[f]	M > V[c]
Seeks to be held	—	—	M > V[f]
Fusses to	—	F > V[f]	M > V[c]
All behaviors[a]	F > M[d]	F > V[d]	M > V[f]

[a]MANOVA comparisons.
[b]$p < .005$.
[c]$p < .001$.
[d]$p < .05$.
[e]$p < .10$.
[f]$p < .01$.
[g]Excluding time that infant was being held.
Note: F = father; M = mother; V = visitor.
Source: Compiled by the author.

baby to the group data. Since there were no significant differences between the
7- and 8- or between the 12- and 13-month visits, the data from these pairs of
visits were combined.

The rates were entered into a repeated measures multivariate analysis of
variance (MANOVA), which showed significant differentiation of the mother,
father, and visitor centroids. Further MANOVAs then compared the mothers
with the fathers, the mothers with the visitor, and the fathers with the visitor.

TABLE 2.2

Patterns of Preferences in the Display of Attachment and Affiliative Behaviors with No Covariate: 12- and 13-Month-Olds

Behaviors	Mother versus Father	Father versus Visitor	Mother versus Visitor
Affiliative behaviors[a]	F > M[b]	F > V[c]	V > M[d]
Smiles	F > M[e]	F > V[d]	V > M[d]
Vocalizes	F > M[e]	F > V[e]	—
Looks	F > M[c]	—	V > M[f]
Laughs	F > M[c]	F > V[e]	—
Proffers	—	F > V[d]	—
Attachment behaviors[a]	—	F > V[e]	M > V[e]
Approaches	—	—	—
Proximity[g]	—	F > V[e]	M > V[c]
Reaches to	—	F > V[c]	M > V[d]
Touches	—	F > V[e]	M > V[e]
Seeks to be held	—	F > V[e]	M > V[e]
Fusses to	—	F > V[e]	M > V[e]
All behaviors [a]	F > M[b]	F > V[c]	M > V[e]

[a]MANOVA comparisons.
[b]$p < .01$.
[c]$p < .005$.
[d]$p < .05$.
[e]$p < .001$.
[f]$p < .10$.
[g]Excluding time that infant was being held.
Note: F = father; M = mother; V = visitor.
Source: Compiled by the author.

Table 2.1 shows the results of the multivariate analyses and the respective univariate comparisons for the early series.

Careful inspection of the results indicates that preferences for both parents over the visitor occurred reliably only in the display of the attachment behaviors. In none of these measures was there a preference for the visitor over either parent. Affiliative interaction with the visitor, on the other hand, was extensive and on some measures exceeded the extent of mother-infant interaction, however, note that while affiliative behaviors were much more likely to be directed to the fathers, there was only one marginally significant preference for the fathers in the display of the attachment behaviors. The other measures showed no preference for either parent. The absence of preferences in the display of attachment behaviors is the most significant and interpretable finding. It indicates that the babies were "equally attached" to both parents. There was certainly no evidence to support the popular presumption that infants of this age should prefer—indeed be uniquely attached to—their mothers.

The data gathered in the later series (that is, the 12- and 13-month observations) were remarkably consistent with this conclusion, and these results appear in Table 2.2.

Again, a repeated measures MANOVA showed significant differentiation of the mother, father, and visitor centroids. Subsequent analyses showed significant preferences for the fathers over the mothers, and mothers over the visitor, and the fathers over the visitor.

As in the early series, preferences for the parents over the visitor were consistent and most marked in the display of the attachment behaviors. Many more affiliative behaviors were directed to the visitor than to the mothers. Most important, there were no preferences for either parent over the other in the display of attachment behaviors.

During the two later visits we monitored and tabulated the frequency with which the adults vocalized to the babies in order to index the relative activity of the adults in interaction with the infants. We found that both parents spoke to the infants much more than the visitor did, and it seems reasonable to predict that their greater activity affected the infants' behavior. Consequently, the analyses were repeated using the frequency of adult vocalization as a covariate. As Table 2.3 shows, the pattern of preferences was similar when this procedure was followed. The covariation procedure had the greatest impact on preferences for the parents over the visitor in the display of affiliative behaviors. It left preferences in the display of attachment behaviors essentially unchanged and made little difference to the mother-father comparison.

In summary, throughout the latter part of the first year of life, both parents were preferred to the visitor in the display of attachment behaviors; this finding also provides an internal check on the validity of the measures. Neither parent was preferred to the other in the display of attachment behaviors. This pattern of preferences was remarkably consistent across time, strongly suggesting that these infants were attached to both their mothers and fathers in the first year of life.

Additional analyses were performed to determine whether separation and reunion behaviors reflected preferences for mothers, as attachment theory would predict. The relevant analysis was detailed, differentiating among several possible separation and reunion responses and taking into account the length of time the adult was out of the room, who was left with the child, and the behavior of the returning adult. The method and the results are not presented in detail because

TABLE 2.3

Patterns of Preferences in the Display of Attachment and Affiliative Behaviors with Frequency of Adult Vocalization as Covariate: 12- and-13-Month-Olds

Behavior	Mother versus Father	Father versus Visitor	Mother versus Visitor
Affiliative behaviors[a]	F > M[b]	—	—
Smiles	F > M[c]	—	V > M[d]
Vocalizes	F > M[c]	—	—
Looks	F > M[b]	—	V > M[d]
Laughs	F > M[b]	F > V[b]	—
Proffers	—	—	—
Attachment behaviors[a]	—	F > V[b]	M > V[c]
Approaches	—	—	—
Proximity[e]	—	F > V[b]	—
Reaches to	—	—	—
Touches	—	F > V[c]	M > V[c]
Seeks to be held	—	F > V[f]	M > V[c]
Fusses to	—	F > V[c]	M > V[c]
All behaviors[a]	F > M[f]	—	M > V[c]

[a] MANOVA comparisons.
[b] $p < .05$.
[c] $p < .005$.
[d] $p < .10$.
[e] Excluding time that infant was being held.
[f] $p < .01$.
Note: F = father; M = mother; V = visitor.
Source: Compiled by the author.

the conclusion they imply is the same as that supported by the previous findings. None of these measures showed significant preferences for either parent at any time during the first year (see Lamb 1975b).

The Second Longitudinal Study

Encouraged by these provocative findings, effort was made to study these children for an additional year. Six of the families declined to participate in the next phase; six infants of comparable background and age were thus recruited. The 20 infants in the "new" sample were observed at home in circumstances similar to those described earlier, when they were 15, 18, 21, and 24 months of age. Detailed information about the procedure and interobserver and intercoder reliabilities have been published elsewhere (Lamb 1977b). In general, the reliability coefficients were comparable to those obtained in the first study.

Data concerning the display of attachment and affiliative behaviors in the second year were analyzed by means of repeated measures of multivariate and univariate analyses of variance procedures. Findings concerning preferences among the three adults (mother, father, and visitor) were only partially consistent with earlier findings concerning infant preferences during the first year of life. As Table 2.4 reveals, the attachment behavior measures again clearly and consistently discriminated between the parents and the visitor. The affiliative behavior measures did not consistently show preferences for familiar (parents) over unfamiliar (visitor) persons. Unexpectedly, however, the mother-father comparison revealed marked and consistent preferences for fathers over mothers in the display of both attachment and affiliative measures. These preferences were evident throughout the second year of life and remained significant even when the relative activity of the adults was taken into account by covariation.

To determine whether each infant had a preferred attachment figure, we asked whether the infant showed a preference for a particular parent on at least four of the six attachment behavior measures. This analysis revealed that the overall preferences for fathers disguised a markedly significant sex difference. An increasing proportion of the boys in the sample showed strong preferences on the attachment behavior measures for their fathers, whereas the girls were unpredictable: some preferred their fathers, some their mothers, and some neither parent (Lamb 1977c). One indication of what might have caused these especially marked preferences on the part of boys is evident in Figure 2.1.

The data in this figure show that the fathers were making themselves particularly salient to their sons. The boys, in turn, responded by paying special attention to—demonstrating preferences for—their fathers. These data may be extremely important. They appear to illustrate the beginning of same-sex modeling—the process of identification that facilitates early gender-identity and gender-role acquisitions. Three facts underline their potential importance: (1) Money's evidence defining the first two to three years as critical for the development of gender identity (Money and Ehrhardt 1972); (2) the evidence that boys whose fathers are absent during the first few years of their lives are especially likely to have difficulties establishing appropriate gender roles (see reviews by Hetherington and Deur 1971; Biller 1971, 1974); and (3) the fact that fathers tend to be more concerned than mothers about the manifestation of sex-appropriate behavior—especially by their sons (Bronfenbrenner 1961a; Goodenough 1957; Heilbrun 1965; Sears, Maccoby, and Levin 1957; Tasch 1955). Meanwhile, a good deal of evidence suggests (as do our data) that sex-differentiating processes commence later and are less

TABLE 2.4

Patterns of Preferences in the Display of Attachment
and Affiliative Behaviors:
15- to-24-Month-Olds

Behavior	Mother versus Father	Father versus Visitor	Mother versus Visitor
Affiliative behaviors[a]	$F > M^b$	$F > V^c$	$V > M^b$
Smiles	$F > M^b$	$F > V^c$	$V > M^c$
Vocalizes	$F > M^c$	$F > V^b$	$M > V^b$
Looks	$F > M^b$	—	$V > M^c$
Laughs	$F > M^b$	$F > V^b$	—
Proffers	$F > M^b$	—	$V > M^d$
Attachment behaviors[a]	$F > M^b$	$F > V^b$	$M > V^b$
Proximity[e]	—	$F > V^b$	$M > V^b$
Touches	$F > M^f$	$F > V^c$	$M > V^b$
Approaches	$F > M^f$	$F > V^b$	$M > V^d$
Seeks to be held	$F > M^c$	$F > V^b$	$M > V^b$
Fusses	—	$F > V^b$	$M > V^b$
Reaches	$F > M^c$	$F > V^b$	—
All behaviors[a]	$F > M^b$	$F > V^c$	$M > V^b$

[a]MANOVA comparisons.
[b]$p < .001$.
[c]$p < .01$.
[d]$p < .05$.
[e]Excluding time that infant was being held.
[f]$p < .10$.
Note: F = father; M = mother; V = visitor.
Source: Compiled by the author.

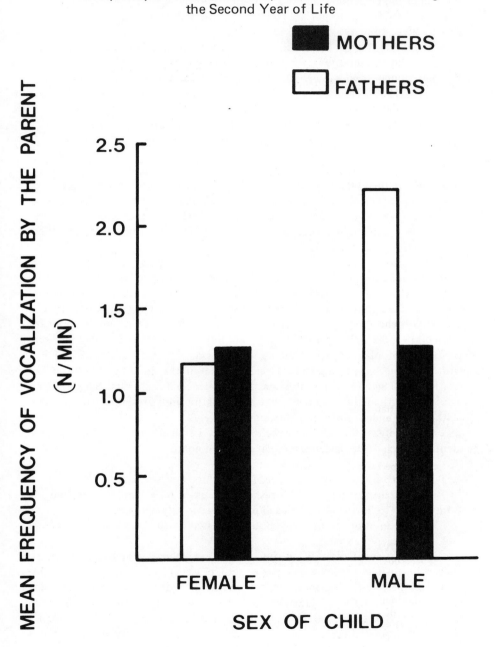

FIGURE 2.1

Frequency of Vocalizations by Parents to Infants During
the Second Year of Life

■ MOTHERS

□ FATHERS

Source: Constructed by the author.

intense among young girls (compare Biller 1976; Brown 1956, 1957, 1958). The most striking thing about our data, though, is that they show fathers becoming especially important to their sons, not from the fourth or fifth year of life, as Freud and other personality development theorists propose, but from the beginning of the second year of life. This suggests that fathers and mothers play qualitatively different roles in early personality development. The next two sections present additional support for this suggestion.

Qualitative Aspects of Mother- and Father-Infant Relations

The data on the occurrence of attachment and affiliative behaviors and separation and reunion responses permit answers only to the first group of questions posed in the introduction: (1) Are infants attached to their fathers as well as to their mothers? (2) Do they become attached to their mothers sooner? (3) Do they consistently prefer their mothers? Certainly, the answers to these questions are quite unequivocal.

The fact that babies are attached to both parents, however, could be relatively unimportant if one relationship is redundant. The implicit assumption of those who had urged that attention be focused on the father-infant relationship was that the father-child relationship is qualitatively different—that it involves different types of experiences and, hence, has different implications for the child's personality development. To test this hypothesis, analyses were performed of play and physical contact interaction in the first year of life, with researchers expecting to find evidence that mother-infant and father-infant relationships involve different sorts of experiences for infants. Such findings would strengthen the argument that both relationships are important and that neither is redundant since they differ qualitatively.

To analyze the play interactions (see Lamb 1976b, 1977a), we first identified each of the instances of play; we then noted:

1. with whom the play occurred;

2. the nature of the baby's response, assessed on a 7-point scale (ranging from 1 = cry to 7 = laugh) with each point behaviorally defined;

3. the duration of the play bout expressed in the number of 15-second units over which it extended;

4. the type of play. We distinguished five categories in the early series: conventional (that is, peek-a-boo, pat-a-cake), physical (that is, rough-and-tumble type), minor physical (that is, tickle games), toy-mediated (all games involving stimulation by toys), and idiosyncratic (all instances of play not classifiable in any of the other four categories). In the later series, the toy-mediated category was divided into three subcategories: stimulus type play (where a toy was

jiggled or operated to stimulate the child directly); ball play (involving reciprocal exchange of a ball-like object); and parallel play (where the two persons engaged in similar activity without real interactions, though mutual participation was necessary for the activity to continue). In the early series, all toy play was stimulus type. In addition, the idiosyncratic category was subdivided into reading, verbal/facial, and others in the later series; and

5. who initiated the play. However, since all the play sequences in the early series and 80 to 90 percent of those in the later series were initiated by the adult, this measure provided no useful information about mother- and father-infant relations.

Although neither parent engaged in more play than the other, the average response to play with the fathers was significantly more positive than with the mothers or the visitor in both the early and later series. The probable reason for this is evident in Figures 2.2 and 2.3, which depict the patterns of play with the mothers and fathers.

It is apparent that the mothers and fathers engaged in different types of play with their infants. Throughout the first year, the mothers were slightly but not significantly more likely to initiate conventional and toy-mediated games, while the fathers were more likely to initiate physically stimulating and idiosyncratic types of play—that is, types of play to which the infants were particularly responsive. The mothers and fathers were thus likely to engage in differentiable types of play with their babies. The differences in the level of average response were much more closely related to the type of play than to the identity of the adult and do not imply anything about parental preference. Nevertheless, these data provide a partial explanation for the consistent preferences for the fathers in the display of affiliative behaviors. These measures seem particularly dependent on immediate dyadic variables (such as the behavior of the partner), whereas the attachment behavior measures are less affected by such parameters (Lamb 1976e, 1977a).

Further analyses were performed on measures of physical contact of holding—a type of interaction that is even more common than play and that, given the emphasis of attachment theory on proximity- and contact-seeking behavior, has great significance in the eyes of attachment theorists. When this analysis was initiated, Ainsworth (personal communication) predicted a preference for the mothers.

Physical contact was recorded each time the infant's weight was supported completely by an adult. For each such instance, we noted by whom the baby was held; the duration of the hold; the baby's response, measured on a 7-point scale similar to that used to assess the response to play; and the purpose of the hold. In the early series, we differentiated six purposes: caretaking, soothing, play, affection, discipline (that is, taking the baby away from forbidden sites),

FIGURE 2.2

Types of Parent-Infant Play Observed in
Seven- and Eight-Month-Old Infants

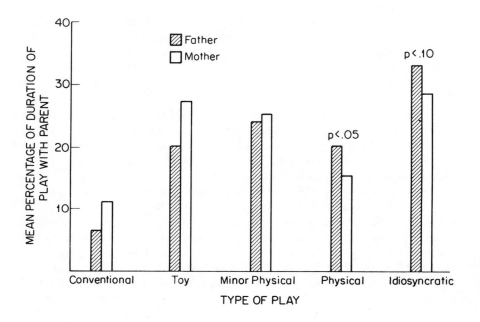

Source: Constructed by the author.

and a residual category, other, which in the later series was subdivided into other
and respondent—picking up the baby because it wanted to be held.

Although the mothers held the babies more than the father in the early
series, the average response to the fathers was significantly more positive. In
fact, thought, as Figures 2.4 and 2.5 show, mothers held the babies for different
reasons than motivated the fathers. The mothers held the babies to perform
caretaking functions and to restrict them (discipline) more often than the
fathers did, whereas the fathers most often held them to play. When the play
holds were excluded, the average response to the two parents did not differ,
suggesting again that the level of response was more strongly related to the
type of play than to the identity of the person involved. As Figure 2.4 (presenting data from the early series) and 2.5 (presenting data from the later series)
show, furthermore, the pattern was remarkably consistent across time.

To summarize, the data suggest that there are significant differences in the types of play and physical contact interaction that infants have with their mothers and fathers—differences that are consistent across time. Considered together, the results of these analyses and of the analyses of attachment and affiliative behaviors suggest that infants are attached to both parents from early in life and that the mother-infant and father-infant relationships differ qualitatively. The fact that the mother- and father-infant relationships involve different types of interaction is important, for it suggests that mothers and fathers provide babies with different kinds of experiences and, hence, that they probably have different roles to play in the children's sociopersonality development. In addition, of course, as attachment figures and sources of security, the two parents play similar roles in their children's development.

FIGURE 2.3

Types of Parent-Infant Play Observed in 12- and 13-Month-Old Infants

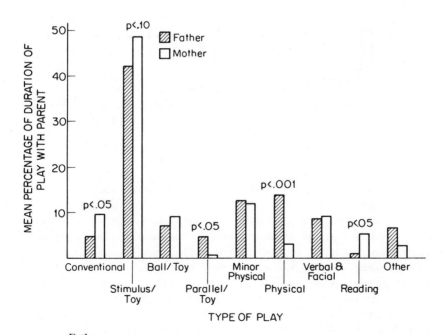

Father
Mother
Source: Contructed by the author.

FIGURE 2.4

Differences between Mothers and Fathers in Their Reasons
for Holding Their Infants at Seven and Eight Months

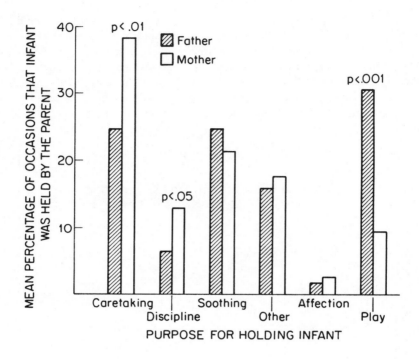

Source: Contructed by the author.

The Effects of Stress on Parental Preferences

In the analyses of attachment behavior, the goal was to determine
whether infants appeared to be attached to their fathers as well as to their
mothers. The answer to this question was consistent: throughout the first
year attachment behavior measures showed no preference for either parent
over the other, whereas during the second year, there emerged preferences
for fathers over mothers—at least among some of the infants.

The question of preference is a troublesome one, however, and merits
further attention. The evidence from the home observations demonstrates
quite convincingly that male toddlers prefer to interact with their fathers—
at least during the times that we observed them. This qualification is

FIGURE 5

Differences between Mothers and Fathers in Their Reasons
for Holding Their Infants at 12 and 13 Months

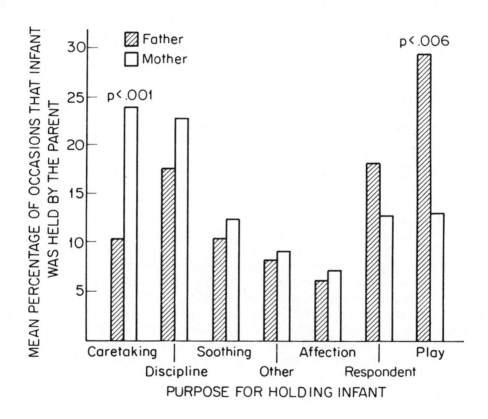

Source: Contructed by the author.

extremely important. Proponents of the ethological attachment theory hold that true preferences cannot be assessed definitively when the attachment behavioral system is not activated. The crucial test of preference, they maintain, is the following: when the attachment behavior system is activated—for example, when the infant is distressed—to whom are the attachment behaviors directed? They point out that when the system is not highly activated, attachment behaviors may be distributed among attachment figures fairly arbitrarily, but that far greater selectivity is evident when the system is activated. In this section, I want to discuss the results of several additional observations involving the participants from the longitudinal projects. These studies were specifically designed to address issues about parental preference and involved observations in laboratory settings exclusively (Lamb 1976a, 1976d, 1976f, 1977b). These observations took place when the infants were 8, 12, 18, and 24 months of age. For our present purposes, however, the most interesting results were obtained in the first three of these studies, each of which involved observations of the infants and their parents in both relatively stress-free as well as relatively stressful circumstances.

The major interest of these studies was the effects of stress on parental preference. Attachment theorists propose that in times of stress, infants should focus their attention rather narrowly on their primary attachment figures, while reducing interaction with secondary attachment figures and nonattachment figures. Stress should thus serve to make evident relative preferences that are obscured in stress-free situations. It was necessary to obtain these data, since the findings reported earlier in this chapter were all derived from the observation of infants and parents in the familiar, stress-free, home environment.

Three putative stressors were employed: a strange situation, the appearance of a strange adult, and fatigue or boredom.

The procedure employed in the studies involving 12- and 18-month-olds utilized four nine-minute episodes. In the first, the infants were observed with both their parents present. In the next two, they were observed first with one parent, then with the other. Finally, the infants were observed with their mothers, fathers, and a strange adult present. At both ages, the infants showed no preference for either parent in the display of attachment behaviors in the first episode, although, as in the home observations, more affiliative behaviors were directed toward the fathers. Several of the babies became more irritable in the next two episodes, and this led them to display more attachment behaviors than in the first episode. It is important to note, though, that the babies sought comfort from (that is, directed attachment behaviors to) whichever parent was with them. There were no preferences for either parent in the occurrence of attachment behaviors. In the fourth episode, when the babies were able to choose between two potential sources of security (which they were not able to do in episodes two and three), the babies turned to their mothers rather than to their fathers. There was a significant preference for mothers over fathers in the display of attachment behaviors in this episode. These results clearly indicate that the mothers were, in fact, the primary or preferred attachment figures of these young infants. Besides being compatible with theoretical predictions, furthermore, the results of these laboratory investigations allow us to explain systematically the apparently inconsistent findings of several previous studies (Cohen and Campos 1974; Kotelchuck 1972, 1976; Kotelchuck et al. 1975; Spelke et al. 1973; Ross et al. 1975; Feldman and Ingham 1975). The results of my studies as well as the findings of these other researchers indicate that in stress-free circumstances, babies do not show preferences for either parent. In times of stress, they organize their behavior quite similarly around whichever parent is with them. When both parents are present, however, distressed infants are more likely to seek comfort from their mothers than from their fathers.

This is not true at all ages, however. When they were eight months of age, our subjects were seen in the laboratory for the first time (Lamb 1976d). The procedure employed at this age was somewhat different than that used at 12 and 18 months, but it, too, permitted us to observe the infants' behavior when distressed. At eight months, the infants showed no consistent preference for either parent over the other. Likewise, a study of distressed 24-month-olds (who were not participants in the longitudinal projects) showed that by two years of age preferences are no longer evident (Lamb 1976c). Clearly, then, in our sample preferences for mothers occurred only during a relatively restricted portion of the second year of life. During this period, however, they appear to be characteristic of the majority of infants raised in families with traditional child care and wage-earner roles.

This is an important finding, particularly in light of the results obtained from home observations of these infants. The results point toward an unambiguous and significant interpretation.

Infants appear to form attachments to both of their parents at about the same time. Although there can be no doubt that most infants are attached to both parents, the way they behave under stress indicates that for most infants mothers are primary attachment figures. Presumably, of course, this rather consistent pattern might be different when child care responsibilities are divided in less traditional ways.

The Effects of the Social Context on Dyadic Social Interaction

In addition to the focus on the effects of stress, the laboratory studies just described were designed to show what effect the presence of either parent had on the infant's interaction with the other parent. These 12-, 18-, and 24-month laboratory observations were the first in a series of studies designed to explore the way in which the presence and behavior of third persons affect dyadic inter-actions. Since these studies are described more fully elsewhere (Lamb 1978c), only the major findings obtained through observation of the participants in the longitudinal project will be discussed (Lamb 1976a, 1976f, 1977b).

Each of the procedures involved episodes in which the infants were observed alone with each parent as well as with both parents simultaneously present. We have consistently found that infants engage in more social inter-action with each parent when alone with him/her than when both parents are simultaneously present. The parents, too, pay more attention to the baby when they are alone with it.

In part, this effect is attributable to the fact that, when two persons are present, individuals tend to divide their attention between the two potential interactants, whereas when only one is present, that person becomes the focus of undivided attention. This "distrubutional" effect is operative in individuals of 12 months of age and older (Lamb1976f, 1978a). A second cue is only effective in infants older than 18 months of age (Lamb 1976a, 1977b). This is the tend-ency of infants to respond to the increased amounts of interaction initated by the adults in the dyadic contexts. Twelve-month-old infants do not adjust their behavior in response to variations in the social activity of their interactive partners (Lamb 1976f, 1978a). In more recent research, we are investigating a third potentially powerful social cue to which 18-month-olds are sensitive (Lamb 1978b). This is the perceived accessibility of the parent. The more atten-tion a parent is paying to his/her spouse, it appears the less the baby attempts to interact with her/him.

In the present context, these studies are important as reminders that the mother-infant and father-infant dyads are components of the family triad; it will be necessary to determine how each of the dyads relates to the larger group and how the relationships between each pair of individuals affect their mode of interaction with others and the way others treat them. Both experi-mental and correlational strategies must be employed in future explorations of these "indirect" or "second order" effects.

CONCLUSION

The findings of the longitudinal studies argue strongly against the con-tinuation of exclusive research focus on mother-infant relations. Evidently, infants are attached from the earliest age to both parents, and the two rela-tionships differ qualitatively. Fathers are not merely occasional mother-sub-stitutes: they interact with their infants in a unique and differentiable way. This makes it probable that the two relationships have differential consequences or implications for personality development. Given our theories concerning the different roles of mothers and fathers in the socialization of older children, it appears that differentiable maternal and paternal roles are continuous from early infancy. As with older children, for example, it seems that fathers may be playing an especially important role in facilitiating the development of sex-appropriate behavior in their infants—especially in their sons.

If we are ultimately to explain the process of sociopersonality development, therefore, it will be necessary for us to consider not only the mothers but also fathers (and probably siblings as well) as socializing agents. We will have to appreciate, furthermore, that they are not independent influences, as they all interact with and affect one another in complex ways. Consequently, it is essential to consider the family system as an interactive whole within which the earliest socialization takes place. Only by acknowledging the complexity and multidimensionality of the infant social world are we likely to comprehend the role of this social environment in the development of personality. Clearly, the research presented in this volume represents only the beginning of an evanescent trend toward a reconceptualization of the nature and process of sociopersonality development in infancy.

3

THE FAMILY IN EARLY INFANCY: SOCIAL INTERACTIONAL AND ATTITUDINAL ANALYSES

Ross D. Parke
Douglas B. Sawin

Our research program has focused on the father's role in early infancy and represents a descriptive attempt to delineate the behavior patterns of fathers and their infants (Parke and Sawin 1975; Sawin and Parke 1975). Mothers are employed as well—but for us, mothers are a control group. In these earlier studies on parental roles in the newborn period, we focused on comparisons of fathers' and mothers' behavior in interactions with their neonates in a feeding context (Parke and O'Leary 1976; Parke and Sawin 1975, 1977). Based on frequencies and durations of caregiving and affection-giving behaviors, we have noted only a few differences that indicate a role differentiation between mothers and fathers during the first days of infant life. Further, assessments of parental responsiveness to infant cues have indicated that fathers and mothers are equally competent in meeting infant needs during feeding (Parke and Sawin 1975, 1976).

The implications of these findings are that fathers appear to have the basic competence to be effective contributors to infant care and that fathers' involvement in these activities can, and perhaps ought to be, an integral component of the infant's early social environment (Parke and Sawin 1976, 1977; Sawin and Parke 1976). However, these findings are only a beginning toward a comprehensive understanding of the father's role in the infant's enduring social environment. First, generalizability of these findings for early paternal behavior across

Support for this project was provided by a grant from the Grant Foundation to Ross D. Parke and a grant from the National Institute of Mental Health (Small Grant, MH 26701-01) to Douglas B. Sawin. Preparation of this paper was supported by Training Grant, HD 00244. Thanks to Brenda Congdon for her preparation of this chapter.

contexts and time are limited since the data were obtained only during feeding sessions in a hospital context and the first three days of infant life. Second, we had not assessed perceptions, congitions, knowledge, values, and attitudes about infants and parenting and the role of these cognitions in the interactive processes among family members (Parke 1978).

The main assumptions underlying our current work can be easily summarized. First, we assume that fathers as well as mothers play an important role in early infancy. Second, we assume that important information can be gained about the development of parent-infant interaction by beginning our observations in the hospital and then continuing them in the home. Not only are there developmental shifts in parent-infant interaction patterns that need to be detailed, but other evidence (Klaus and Kennell 1976; Lind 1974) suggests that the early opportunities for interaction may shape later patterns of interactions.

Under the influence of attachment theory, the focus of much prior research has been on the post-six-months-of-age period, since it was assumed that the infant could only form an attachment with the parent after the achievement of object permanence. However, we recognize that for parents, it is hardly necessary for the parent to wait six months to achieve "object permanence." Therefore, the problem becomes redefined as the way in which parents—fathers and mother—adjust and adapt to their new infant and the role of the infant in this adaptive process. In addition, by focusing on the preattachment phase, some clues concerning the determinants of infant attachment may be forthcoming.

Moreover, by explicitly recognizing the parent as a thinking organism, it becomes clear that studies of parent-infant interaction must consider the impact of parental cognitions, preceptions, attitudes, and knowlege on the interactive process (Parke 1978). Implicit in many previous models of interaction is the assumption that the parent reacts to the behavior of the infant in a mechanical or unthinking fashion. This is, in large measure, a legacy of our stimulus-response (S-R) heritage, which has led us to ignore the role of subjective events in an effort to develop an objective analysis of interaction patterns.

Nor has the recent trend of replacing our S-R language with the assumptions of a biologically derived ethological approach resulted in any correction of this denial of cognitive factors in social interaction. Another explanation for our failure to consider parent's cognitions may be that, in our enthusiasm to give the infant proper recognition as a contributor to the interactive process, we have oversimplified our assumptions concerning the partner's relative capacities in the dyadic exchange by treating them as coacting equals. Unfortunately, the implicit assumption may have inadvertently slipped in that the cognitive capacities of the infant and parent could be treated as functionally similar. Although no one would seriously support such a view, we have, in fact, been treating the parent as a black box reactor in the parent-infant interaction context. This failure to treat parents as information-processing organisms is particularly surprising in light of the general cognitive revival within psychology in the past 15 years.

One other reason for the limited consideration of cognition variables in current theoretical conceptualizations of parent-infant interaction is the failure to distinguish adequately between parental reports as objective measures of parental behavior and parental reports as indexes of parental knowledge, attitudes, stereotypes, and perceptions. These latter classes of variables are legitimate and important sources of data in their own right and are not easily derivable from observation alone. These types of parental reports provide information about ways in which parents preceive, organize, and understand both their infants and their roles as parents. The assumption is that these cognitive sets serve as filters through which the objective behaviors of the infant are processed. It is not assumed that parent perceptions of infant behavior are shorthand routes to circumvent the task of directly observing the infant. Rather it is assumed these perceptions, attitudes, and values are different and to some degree independent sources of data. In fact, it is probably a mistake to assume that actual and preceived behaviors are necessarily similar and can be treated as isomorphic sources of information (Tulkin and Cohler 1973).

Another assumption in our current work concerns the mutual regulatory nature of the parent-infant interaction process. The earlier phases of unidirectional models, whereby researchers focused only on the parent's impact on the infant, is finally behind us (Lewis and Rosenblum 1974). However, in an enthusiasm to correct this historical imbalance, a new focus on the infant's impact on the parent has occurred instead of the more appropriate focus on the reciprocal nature of the interactive process. A more balanced perspective, however, entails the study of reciprocity in interaction. The ways in which parents and infants mutually influence and regulate each other are of central interest.

The purpose of this chapter is to deal with these issues by presenting preliminary findings from a recently completed short-term longitudinal study of parent-infant interactions over three months beginning at birth. The focus of the findings is on the interrelations among patterns of behavior in parent-infant interactions, characteristics of the parents and infants, and parents' attitudes, knowledge, and feelings about the baby.

In approaching these issues we have adopted a model of the family unit as a system of reciprocal and interacting influences that change over time. Not only does this system consist of the three interacting members—mother, father, and infant—but each member brings a set of components to the system—components such as behavioral styles in interactions, past experience, and learning, characteristics such as age and sex, and a variety of individual differences. For the parents, additional factors such as role attitudes, values, knowledge about infants, and feelings about the infant are also considered. This approach reflects our view that multiple measures and levels of analyses are necessary to understand social interaction (Hartup 1979; Parke 1979b).

METHOD

Overview

Mothers and fathers were observed interacting with their infants at three time periods: at early postpartum in the hospital, at three weeks in the home, and at three months in the home. Each time observations of mother-infant and father-infant interaction were made while each parent bottle fed the infant for ten minutes and played with the infant with a toy for five minutes. In addition, for each period, parents completed questionnaires designed to tap knowledge about and attitudes toward infants.

Participants

Forty infants and their mothers and fathers participated in the study. All families were white. The sample consisted of 20 girls and 20 boys; half of each sex were first-born infants and half were later-born infants. All infants were full term and judged normal and healthy by their pediatricians. Apgar scores for all infants were seven and above at one minute and eight and above at five minutes. All infants were bottle fed.

The mothers ranged in age from 17 to 34 years with a mean age of 25 years, while fathers ranged from 19 to 38 with a mean age of 27 years. The Hollingshead Two Factor Index of Social Position was used to describe socio-economic status. The social class of the sample families ranged from Class I to Class V with the following distribution:

Social Class

	I	II	III	IV	V
Number of Families	2	6	15	13	4

In summary, the sample is broadly representative with the majority of participants being middle class.

The majority of fathers (36) completed high school and many (24) had at least some college training. Similarly, most of the mothers had completed high school (36) and some (16) had completed some college level education. Most of the mothers in our study were not employed during the early phases of the investigation. However, a small number (6) of mothers were working either part- or full-time at the time of the third observation.

Assessments

Observational assessments

All observations were made by trained observers, who recorded a wide range of parental and infant behaviors. These behaviors are listed in Table 3.1. All behaviors were precoded by a three digit number and were recorded in sequence of their occurrence by the observer using a portable electronic recorder. The recording device, a Model DAK-8 DataMyte is a ten-button, audible tone keyboard that stores coded digital information on a cassette tape recorder. In turn, by transferring the tape to a coupler, a printout of precoded behaviors in their order and time of occurrence (in seconds) is obtained. This observation system yields data regarding the frequency of occurrence of each parent and infant behavior and the duration of each infant and parent behavior. This information permits computaion of the degree of contigency between infant and caretaker behavior. Specifically, two sets of sequences are derived from the interaction data: infant-elicited parent behavior, whereby the probability of occurrence of various parental behaviors are determined in response to an infant signal (that is, vocalizing, moving, et cetera) and parent-elicited infant behavior, whereby the probability of occurrence of various infant behaviors is assessed in response to various parental behaviors (for example, touch, rock, vocalize, smile, et cetera). A time boundary of ten seconds after the occurrence of the behavior of one individual defined a contingent response on the part of either infant or parent.

Reliabilities for each parent and infant behavior were calculated on an intermittent basis throughout the data collection phase. Reliability, as assessed by Pearson product moment correlations ranged from .70 to .99 for the behaviors reported in this chapter.

Parent questionnaire

A 45-item questionnaire developed by Parke and Sawin (1975) was completed separately by mothers and fathers at each time point. Separate versions were developed for mothers and fathers. The questionnaires were designed to assess parental attitudes toward infants, their knowledge about infant development, and their perceptions of their parental role. The questionnaires consisted of statements to which the parent responded on a five-point scale from strongly agree to strongly disagree. A principal-component factor analysis, using data from 100 mothers and 100 fathers yielded six distinct factors. This factor structure was replicated in a later analysis, using 160 fathers and 159 mothers. The

TABLE 3.1

Categories of Parent and Infant Behaviors

Activity	Parent Behaviors	Infant Behaviors
Auditory	Vocalize to baby Imitate baby vocalization Vocalize to someone else Present auditory stimulus, for example, a toy	Vocalize Negative Vocalization Sneeze, spit up, cough
Caregiving	Pat or rub baby to burp Miscellaneous caretakeing of baby Wipe face, hands, bottom	n.a.
Caretaking	n.a.	Emits loud, distinct burp noise
Feeding	Feed bottle Stimulate feeding	Feeding by bottle Sucks thumb or hand Makes sucking noise
Holding	Pick up baby Hold close Hold far or loose Hold with neutral contact Walking with baby	n.a.
Tactile	Rock or bounce Kiss Touch with toy Other touching Variation in touching	Clings to parent Holds object
Visual	Look at infant Look more intensely Smile Make face at baby Imitate or mimic baby Show toy or object Change visual stimulus Look elsewhere	Look at parent Smile Make face or mouth movements

n.a.: not applicable
Source: Compiled by authors.

six factors can be described briefly. A first factor, parental strain, was composed of items such as resentment concerning how long it takes to feed the baby, how demanding babies are, having to give up favorite activities for the baby, how much attention babies require; disappointment about the baby not behaving like other babies, and about having had the baby at this time in the parents' lives; anxiety and worry about the infant not being active enough, about the strain the infant would place on family finances, and about how difficult it is to calm the baby when he/she is fussy. This factor accounted for 43 percent of the variance. A second factor, which accounted for 18 percent of the variance, concerned the parent's attitudes about affectionate stimulation for the infant and included such items as frequency of holding the baby, pleasure from holding the baby, enjoyment of infant feeding time, feeling that cuddling is good for babies and that diapering is a good time to play with the baby, and the value of verbal stimulation for the infant's development. A third factor, the parent's concern for infant happiness, included such items as babies smile when they are happy, babies are happiest when being held, and it is good to smile at babies. This factor accounted for 12 percent of the variance. Another factor labeled "caregiving anxiety" accounted for approximately 10 percent of the questionnaire variance. This factor tapped such parental concerns as "I'm nervous about holding my baby" and "I'm afraid of hurting my infant." A fifth factor, which tapped 9 percent of the variance, concerned parental knowledge of infant visual competence. This factor included such items as babies can distinguish the different parts of people's faces, babies can following a moving object with their eyes, babies are able to differentiate between people, and parents plan to use toys to play with their infants. A sixth and final factor concerned parental role attitudes. This factor included items such as "mothers should be solely responsible for infant care," "it is not father's role to caretake infant," and "father's main responsibility is to play." This factor accounted for 8 percent of the questionnaire variance.

Procedure

Father-infant and mother-infant interactions were observed in the hospital (mean [$\bar{X}$] age of infant at the first observation was four to six hours) and again at home when the infants were three weeks and three months old. At each time point mother and father were observed separately. The order of father-infant and mother-infant observations was counterbalanced.

Parent-infant interaction was observed in two different contexts, feeding and playing at each of the three time points. Feeding was observed for ten minutes and parents were told to "go ahead and feed your infant in whatever is your normal way." At the completion of feeding, which typically lasted 20 to 30 minute, the observer introduced the "play" phase. The parents were informed that we would like to watch them while they played with their infant. Specifically, the parents were handed a small, rattle-type toy without any specific instructions concerning how the toy was to be used and told, "Do whatever you want—I will watch for five minutes and see how the baby responds." The toy, marketed commercially under the name "Clickee," consists of brightly colored plastic discs on a loop.

The mother-infant and father-infant observations were made at separate feeding sessions and generally on a different day in the case of the home visits. Following each observation session, the observed parent completed the questionnare.

RESULTS

Frequency and Duration of Observed Parent Behaviors with Infants

The frequencies and durations of the parents' behaviors in interaction with their infants will be presented for four classes of parenting activities: (1) visual attending (that is, parent looks at the infant; parent looks intensely or more closely at the infant), (2) routine care and grooming (that is, routine care-giving—parent checks diapers, adjusts bunting or clothing, combs or brushes hair; parent wipes the baby's face or hands), (3) affection giving (that is, parent holds baby close/snugly; parent smiles; parent kisses baby), and (4) stimulation (that is, tactual-kinesthetic—parent touches or moves part of baby; visual—parent mimics the baby's facial expressions or shows the baby a toy; auditory—parent vocalizes/talks to the baby or parent juggles or rattles toy to make sounds for the baby). The frequencies and durations for each of the parent behaviors during the feeding sessions and during the play sessions were submitted to 2 x 2 x 2 x 3 analyses of variance to assess the effects due to parent gender, infant gender, ordinal position of infant (first-born versus later-borns) and time (hospital, three weeks, three months).

Four issues will be explored from the findings of these analyses. First, we will examine differences between mothers and fathers that were stable over time, infant gender, and infant ordinal position, and that thus suggest consistent role differentiation and characteristic parenting styles for mothers and fathers. Second, we will examine the differences between mothers' and fathers' behaviors in interaction with their infants that are attributable to the modifying influences of the infant's gender and ordinal position. Third, we will look at the general changes over time in parenting practices, which are similar for mothers and fathers and which suggest the influence of practice and infant development on parent behavior. and, finally, we will examine differences between mothers and father in the ways their behavior changes over time and, thus, the ways their parenting roles differentially shift and evolve as the parents have more experience with each other and with their infant.

Overview

In general, the similarities and differences in patterns of parenting between mothers and fathers that we have observed in earlier studies were evident in the hospital observations of the present study. However, the inclusion of the play sessions and the longitudinal assessments in this study confirm our predictions that factors associated with context and with time over the first few months are important determinants of evolving patterns of parent-infant interactions and the development of characteristic styles of parenting. First, there are a number of shifts in the frequency and durations of parenting behaviors over time that are similar for both mothers and fathers. Second, there are also a number of differences between mothers and fathers that hold across time. Third, infant gender plays a more important role in accounting for parent differences than our early findings indicated, whereas infant ordinal position appears to be a less important determinant of mother-father differences than previously observed in the perinatal period. And, finally, differences between mothers and fathers show significant shifts over time that are characterized by role reversals and role convergence suggesting the operation of reciprocal influences of mothers and fathers on each other over time, experience, and infant development.

Changing Patterns of Parenting Over Time: Similarities Between Mothers and Fathers

First, the changes over time in parenting behaviors that are similar for mothers and fathers will be examined. Main effects for the time factor indicate that parents of young infants engage in less routine care and grooming as the infant grows older. Both the frequency of routine caretaking during feeding—$F(2,72) = 10.61, p < .01$; $X = 1.74, .75$, and $.68$—and the frequency of this behavior during the play sessions decreased across time, $F(2,72) = 9.84, p < .01$; $\bar{X} = .89, .30$, and $.34$. Similarly, the frequency of parents wiping their infant's face and hands decreased from birth to three months, $F(2,72) = 1.14, p < .001$; $\bar{X} = 4.49, 2.85$, and 2.18.

Affectionate behavior by parents toward their infants showed similar decreases over time for the parent variable "holds close"—$F(2,72) = 43.32, p < .01$; $\bar{X} = 2.18, 1.60$, and $.65$— but not for smiling and kissing. Visual attending and stimulation behaviors on the part of parents show no consistent increases or decreases over time that are the same for both parents; rather, these classes of parenting behaviors were characterized by differences between mothers and fathers that were a function of infant gender and experience over time.

To summarize the main effects indicating consistent changes in parents' behavior over time, our data indicate that while parents spend less time giving routine care to their infants and less time holding them close and snugly as the infant matures, parents, as a group, show similar levels of affection in the forms of kissing and smiling. In addition, parents are attentive and provide similar levels of stimulation for their growing infant over the first three months.

To assess the stability of the behavior of individual parents across time, correlations were run between the frequencies and durations of parent behaviors (mothers and fathers separately) across the three observaion points. Very few of the correlations were significant, which suggests that the patterns of stability and change that were revealed in the group analyses may not apply in a simple fashion to the stability of the individual parent's placement in a group of parents. In short, there was little interindividual· continuity across the newborn-to-three-month age period in parental behavior.

Differences Between Mothers and Fathers

There were also differences between mothers and fathers that held over time as indicated by main effects for the parent gender factor. As in our earlier studies, these differences are few and are similar to the parent differences that we have reported from observations made only in the perinatal hospital setting (Parke and O'Leary 1976; Parke and Sawin 1975). Mothers spent more time in routine caregiving (checks/changes diaper, dresses, grooms, covers) with their infants than fathers—frequency: $F(1,36) = 5.33$, $p < .03$; duration: $F(1,36) = 2.93$, $p > .05 < .10$. In another parent difference that favored mothers, kissing the baby was more frequent in the feeding context—$F(1,36) = 6.08$, $p < .02$; $\bar{X}_m = .80$ versus $\bar{X}_f = .25$— for mothers than for fathers. The single main effect that favored fathers was more frequent visual stimulation in the form of mimicking the infant's facial expressions, $F(1,36) = 6.07$, $p < .02$; $\bar{X}_f = .26$ versus $X_m = .08$. Thus, as in our earlier studies, we again see some evidence for role differentiation between parents, with mothers engaging in more routine caretaking (and kissing the baby more often) and fathers engaging in more social stimulation.

Although the correlational analyses of the frequencies of mother and father behavior yielded only a chance level of significant correlations, the analyses of the duration of mother and father behavior yielded a more meaningful picture. Most of the correlations were positive, which indicated that the amount of time spent by mothers and fathers in different parenting activities was similar.

Sex of Infant as a Determinant of Differences
Between Fathers and Mothers

More frequent than main effects for parent gender were interaction effects of this factor with the infant gender. These interaction effects indicate that infant gender plays a role in modifying mothers' and fathers' patterns of interaction with their infants. Further, parent roles, defined by the activities they engage in with their infants during feeding times and play times, are differentiated by infant gender in a complementary way: fathers play a different role with sons than with daughters, while mothers play the reciprocal role to the fathers' with daughters and sons.

First, there were no consistent parent differences associated with infant gender for routine care and grooming; however, for affection-giving behaviors we found that mothers held their sons close and snugly more frequently and for longer periods during play than they did their daughters, $F(1,36) = 5.17$, $p < .03$. Fathers tended to hold their daughters close to them more than their sons (Table 3.2).

In contrast, for visual attending and stimulation behaviors, fathers consistently favored their sons and mothers more often favored their daughters. As Table 3.2 shows, fathers spent less time looking at their daughters than they did at their sons and fathers more frequently looked closely and intently at their sons than at their daughters. Fathers also provided more visual and tactual stimulation for their sons. During the play sessions, fathers presented the toy for their sons to look at more frequently than to their daughters. Fathers touched and moved their sons' arms, legs, and other body parts more than they did their daughters', while mothers showed the reverse pattern, $F(1,36) = 4.94, p < .03$. During feeding, the fathers made more frequent attempts to stimulate their sons' feeding by moving or jiggling the bottle than they did for their daughters. Mothers, on the other hand, more frequently showed the toy to their daughters, touched and moved their daughters more, and made more attempts to stimulate their feeding. Thus, while there is little differentiation in mothers' and fathers' behavior toward their sons and daughters for routine caregiving behaviors, there are indications that mothers' and fathers' affection giving is more focused on their opposite-sexed infant, while their attending and stimulation behaviors are more frequent with their same-sexed infant in such a way that suggests that mothers and fathers play reciprocal and complementary roles with male and female babies.

TABLE 3.2

Means for Selected Categories of Maternal and Paternal Behavior Classified by Sex of Infant

Variable	Fathers		Mothers		F Value Sex of Parent by Sex of Infant Interaction
	Male Infant	Female Infant	Male Infant	Female Infant	
Holds infant close (frequency in play situation)	0.51	0.57	0.78	0.52	5.17†
Looks at infant (duration in feed situation)	571.30	553.40	567.90	570.30	4.10†
Look more closely at infant (frequency in play situation)	11.20	8.80	6.90	8.70	3.79*
Touches or moves infant (frequency in play situation)	6.70	5.50	4.50	7.20	4.94†
Show toy to infant (frequency in play situation)	10.80	8.60	8.60	9.00	3.96†
Stimulates infant to feed (frequency in feed situation)	18.70	14.20	15.20	17.40	4.24†

*$p < .10$.
†$p < .05$.
Note: $df = 1,36$.
Source: Compiled by the authors.

Infant Ordinal Position as a Determinant of Differences Between Fathers and Mothers

Significant interactions of parent gender and infant ordinal position indicate that infant ordinal position differentially affected fathers and mothers. Fathers smiled less frequently while feeding firstborns ($\bar{X} = 6.63$) than later-borns ($X = 8.33$), while mothers smiled more frequently while feeding firstborns ($\bar{X} = 9.50$) than later-borns ($\bar{X} = 7.48$), $F(1,36) = 4.51, p < .04$. In addition, fathers held firstborns close for shorter periods ($\bar{X} = 77.37$) than later-borns ($\bar{X} = 105.30$), while mothers held firstborns close ($\bar{X} = 103.52$) for longer periods than later-borns ($\bar{X} = 83.50$), $F(1,36) = 4.12, p < .05$. Conversely, fathers held firstborns far/loose for longer periods ($\bar{X} = 145.18$) for shorter ($X = 157.52$), while mothers held firstborns far/loose ($X = 145.18$) for shorter periods than later-borns ($\bar{X} = 171.32$), $F(1,36) = 4.44, p < .04$.

Differential Shifts Over Time in Patterns of Mother-Infant and Father-Infant Interaction

Our findings indicate that the direction and magnitude of differences between mothers' and fathers' patterns of parenting changed over the early months of infancy. The analyses of parent behavior yielded a number of interaction effects involving parent gender and time factors. These interaction effects indicate not only differences between mothers' and fathers' behaviors but differential shifts in the roles that mothers and fathers play over time that are associated with the type of activity being engaged in (that is, routine care and affectionate behavior versus infant stimulation) and the context of parenting. That is, the nature of the shifts in parenting roles tended to be different in feeding and play contexts—role reversals with subsequent role convergence were characteristic to time trends in the play context, whereas role reversals that were maintained over subsequent time were more typical in the feeding context.

An example of convergence of mothers' and fathers' behavior in the play sessions is found in the frequency of smiling. Mothers smiled somewhat more than fathers in the hospital setting; fathers smiled more than mothers at three weeks observation; and by three months, the difference between fathers and mothers was the smallest, $F(2,72) = 7.01, p < .01$.

Mother and father comparisons for frequency and duration of routine caretaking (for example, checks diapers, grooms) during the play session at each time point yielded a similar parent-gender-by-time interaction, wherein mothers engaged in more caretaking than fathers during the hospital observation, fathers engaged in more caretaking than mothers during the play session at three weeks observation, and by the time of the three months observation, fathers and mothers in similar amounts of caretaking during play with their infant (see Table 3.3). Compare this trend with the frequencies of parent wiping the infant's

TABLE 3.3

Means for Selected Categories of Maternal and Paternal Behavior at Three Observation Periods

Variables	Fathers			Mothers			F Value		
	Hospital	Three Weeks	Three Months	Hospital	Three Weeks	Three Months	Sex of Parent[1]	Time of Observation[2]	Interaction
Smiles at infant (frequency in play situation)	4.20	5.03	4.23	5.10	3.65	3.73	n. s.	7.01[b]	n. s.
Routine caretaking (frequency in play situation)	1.58	2.95	0.50	2.83	0.40	0.98	n. s.	9.83[b]	3.90[a]
Wipes infant (frequency in feed situation)	3.78	3.15	2.75	5.20	2.45	1.62	n. s.	12.13[b]	5.89[b]
Touches or moves infant (frequency in feed situation)	8.10	5.72	7.12	6.38	8.00	13.02	n. s.	3.89[a]	3.97[a]
Shows infant toy or object (duration in play situation)	264.47	238.10	255.70	232.20	260.15	283.97	n. s.	3.86[a]	5.88[b]
Uses toy or object to make noise (frequency in play situation)	30.27	27.38	27.42	23.13	29.77	28.77	n. s.	n. s	4.01[a]

n. s.: not significant
[a]$p < .05$.
[b]$p < .01$.
Note: $df = 2,72$.

[1]$df = 1,36$
[2]$df = 2,72$
Source: Compiled by the authors.

face or hands during the feeding sessions (Table 3.3). At first observation in the hospital, mothers wiped the baby during the feeding more frequently than the fathers. At the second observation of the feeding sessions at three weeks, there was a small difference between fathers and mothers that favored fathers; by three months, fathers wiped their infant's face or hands during feeding more frequently than mothers, with the difference being greater than at three weeks.

Thus, for routine care and grooming and for affectionate smiling, mothers and fathers show a tendency to reverse roles between the perinatal period and third week, with the role reversal being maintained in the feeding context (that is, "wipes infant") and resulting in a role convergence in the play context (that is, "routine caretaking" and "smiles") by the third month.

These trends for role reversals and convergences were also evident for stimulation behaviors, though the differences between mothers and fathers were in the opposite direction. As indicated in Table 3.3, for parents providing tactual-kinesthetic stimulation for the infant in the feeding session, fathers more frequently touched and moved their infant's in the feeding session, fathers more frequently touched and their infant's hands, legs, and other limbs in the hospital than did mothers. At the three week feeding observation, mothers touched and moved their infants more than fathers with this difference increasing over time and being greatest at the three months feeding observation. Visual stimulation of the infant by the parents during play sessions also showed a parent-gender-by-time interaction. At the earliest play observation, fathers showed the infant the toy more than the mothers, but by three weeks the mothers were showing the toy to their infants more than fathers and continued to do so during the three months visit, but the mother-father difference at this later time was slightly smaller than the reverse difference at the first (three-day) observation (see Table 3.3). Finally, parents providing auditory stimulation for their infants during the play session was characterized by the same trend evident in the other stimulation variables. At time one, fathers more frequently than mothers jiggled or rattled the toy for their infant to hear, but by time two at three weeks, mothers were providing this auditory stimulation more often than fathers; at the three moths visit, the difference between mothers and fathers was very small (see Table 3.3).

Thus, viewed together, these parent-gender-by-time interactions reveal two types of trends in shifting roles of mothers and fathers in their interactions with their infants over the first months of infant life. First, the direction of the differences between mothers and fathers was a function of the type of parenting activity being engaged in, with the time trends indicating a shift from more stereotyped behavior (mothers giving their infants more care and affection than fathers do and fathers giving more stimulation than mothers do) to the opposit roles or more homogeneous roles by three months.

Second, the nature of the function that defines these different trends was determined by the context of parenting. Role reversals were evident in both feeding and play contexts by three weeks, with these reversals being stable into the third month only in the feeding context. In the play context, the role reversals evident at three weeks were characterized by convergence at three months for all but one of the interactions ("shows toy") obtained from the observations in the play context.

These indications of role reversals and convergence suggest that mutual modeling effects may be operating in the family system during the early period of infancy. It appears that as the parents experience the care, affection, and stimulation of their infant together they are adopting the behaviors of their mates, which are reflected in shifts in each other's behavior in the direction that was more characteristic of their mate at an earlier time. Parents may learn from each other and, at the same time, provide a model for each other's learning.

Parent and Infant Responsiveness in Dyadic Interactions: Sequential Analyses Findings

Does the infant become more responsive to parental behavior across the first three months of life? And, second, does the parent become more responsive to infant cues and signals over this same period? To answer these questions, we employed conditional probability analyses that permit the examination of the changes in the probability of occurrence of infant behavior as a function of the occurrence of a given parent behavior (Parke and Sawin 1975; Sawin, Langlois, and Leitner 1977). For our purposes, we asked what changes in probability of a particular infant behavior occur in the ten-second interval following a parent behavior or, alternatively, whether shifts in parent behavior occur in response to an infant behavior. In other words, if a parent emits a behavior, what happens in the next ten-second interval in terms of the infant's behavior?

A brief methodological note is in order. Since behaviors occur with different frequencies throughout an interaction session, it is necessary to determine the unconditional or baseline probabilities of the occurrence of the target infant behavior. To do this, the probability that an infant behavior occurred in each of the 60 ten-second intervals of the interaction session was calculated. If there are no seqential depedencies of any infant behaviors with the parent-trigger behavior (conditional event) in proportion to their unconditional (baseline) occurrence in the total data set.

Two parent modifiers (trigger variables) will illustrate the general pattern of changes. As Table 3.4 shows, parental vocalization is a clear modifier of a variety of infant behaviors in the feeding situation. In response to parental vocalizations, the infant's attention to the parent increases even in the newborn period as well as at the three weeks and three months period. Second, in response to parental vocalization, there is an increase in infant vocalizing; again, this respon-

TABLE 3.4

Comparisons of Baseline and Conditional Probabilities of Parental Vocalizations as Modifiers of Infant Behavior

Infant Behavior	Newborn		Three Weeks		Three Months		F Values		
	Baseline	Conditional	Baseline	Conditional	Baseline	Conditional	Time[a] Point	B/C[b,c]	Interaction
Looks at parent	.08	.38	.1500	.340	.220	.460	7.09	56.91	n. s.
Vocalizes	.11	.38	.2500	.370	.270	.390	8.87	18.79	6.02
Makes face	.18	.45	.0700	.450	.070	.520	n. s.	111.17	7.12
Smiles	.00	.00	.0002	.012	.018	.202	17.83	17.36	17.02

n. s.: not significant
[a] $df = 2,72$.
[b] $df = 1,36$.
[c] B = baseline; C = conditional.
Note: For all F values indicated, $p < .01$.
Source: Compiled by the authors.

siveness to parental auditory stimulation is evident in the newborn period as well as the later time points.

However, there is a general shift in the overall frequency of infant vocalization across the first three months with the infant engaging in more spontaneous (unconditional) vocalization. In contrast, the infant is less likely to exhibit "makes face" (Table 3.4) across the first three months spontaneously but is increasingly likely to do so in response to parental vocalization. Finally, the probability of infant smiles increases markedly in response to parental vocalizations; these are only meaningful for the three month period since the baseline frequency of infant smiles is very low prior to this time point.

Parental smiling behavior—a visual, in contrast to an auditory, stimulatory pattern—is not a consistent elicitor of infant behavior, particularly in the newborn period. As Table 3.5 indicates, smiling is actually an effective inhibitor of infant vocalization but, not surprisingly, has no consistent impact on the infant's attention directed toward the parent. Parental smiling does result in slight increases in infant facial expressions such as "makes face" (Table 3.5) at three weeks and more so at three months but tends to inhibit infant facial expressions in the newborn period. At three months a parent smile increases infant smiling as well. The general pattern was qualified by a parent by baseline over conditional probability interaction of borderline significance, $F(1,36) = 3.00$, $p < .10$. Father smiles were less likely than mother smiles to elicit smiling in infants (father baseline was .005; father conditional was .017; mother baseline was .008; mother conditional was .028). This pattern is further qualified by both ordinal position and sex of infant. Smiling by fathers—$F(1,36) = 4.61$, $p < .05$ for parent by baseline over conditional by infant gender by ordinal position— is most likely to elicit smiling from their first-born boys than from either later-born boys or girls of either ordinal position. In contrast, maternal smiling elicits least smiling in first-born boys and most in later-born boys and first-born girls.

The general pattern of infant reactions to parental vocalizations and smiling that was observed in the feeding situation was evident in the play context as well. Again, both mother and father auditory and visual cues were reliable elicitors of infant behavior.

Do parents become increasingly responsive to infant cure? As Table 3.6 shows, there is a general pattern of increasing responsiveness to infant vocalizations across the first three months of life during feeding. During the newborn period, most parent behaviors show little responsiveness to this particular infant cue. Neither looking more closely, smiling, touching, nor vocalizing on the part of the parent increases in reponse to infant behavior during this period; in contrast, there is a slight inhibitory effect on parental behavior. At three weeks and three months, however, parents look more closely, smile, and touch their infants following an infant vocalization. Parent vocalization remains high throughout this three month period and does not increase in response to infant vocalizing; in fact, parental vocalizations are less likely (that is, are

TABLE 3.5

Comparisons of Baseline and Conditional Probabilities of Parental Smiles as Modifiers of Infant Behavior

Infant Behavior	Newborn		Three Weeks		Three Months		F Values		
	Baseline	Condi-tional	Baseline	Condi-tional	Baseline	Condi-tional	Time[a] Point	B/C[b,c]	Inter-action
Looks at parent	.08	.15	.13	.11	.23	.25	16.40[d]	n. s.	2.84[e]
Vocalizes	.12	.07	.25	.11	.29	.12	26.01[d]	6.14[d]	4.30[e]
Makes face	.18	.14	.09	.13	.07	.15	3.77[f]	n. s.	5.97[d]
Smiles	.00	.00	.00	.00	.02	.10	17.18[d]	11.19[d]	11.27[d]

n. s.: not significant
[a] $df = 2,72$.
[b] $df = 1,36$.
[c] B = baseline; C = conditional.
[d] $p < .01$.
[e] $p < .10$.
[f] $p < .05$.
Source: Compiled by the authors.

TABLE 3.6

Comparisons of Baseline and Conditional Probabilities of Infant Vocalizations as Modifiers of Parental Behaviors

Parent Behavior	Newborn		Three Weeks		Three Months		F Values		
	Baseline	Condi-tional	Baseline	Condi-tional	Baseline	Condi-tional	Time[a] Point	B/C[b,c]	Inter-action
Look close	.10	.10	.11	.25	.11	.22	9.95[d]	13.21[d]	7.91[d]
Vocalize	.42	.10	.38	.21	.44	.25	9.30[d]	44.12[d]	8.53[d]
Touch	.10	.08	.10	.18	.13	.22	8.98[d]	5.34[e]	6.14[e]
Smile	.12	.10	.10	.20	.15	.23	11.25[d]	15.96[d]	2.42

[a] $df = 2,72$.
[b] $df = 1,36$.
[c] B=baseline; C= conditional.
[d] $p < .01$.
[e] $p < .05$.
Source: Compiled by the authors.

TABLE 3.7

Comparisons of Baseline and Conditional Probabilities of Infant Movement as Modifiers of Parental Behaviors

Parent Behavior	Newborn		Three Weeks		Three Months		F Values		
	Baseline	Conditional	Baseline	Conditional	Baseline	Conditional	Time[a] Point	B/C[b,c]	Interaction
Look close	.10	.35	.11	.38	.11	.61	19.68^d	256.22^d	18.73^d
Vocalize	.42	.41	.35	.45	.45	.58	9.81^d	5.38^e	9.95^d
Touch	.10	.42	.10	.38	.15	.52	8.03^d	161.86^d	4.53^e
Smile	.12	.37	.10	.37	.15	.51	7.63^d	151.52^d	3.35^e

[a] $df = 2,72$.
[b] $df = 1,36$.
[c] B = baseline; C = conditional.
[d] $p < .01$.
[e] $p < .05$.
[f] $p < .10$.
Source: Compiled by the authors.

inhibited) after infant vocalizations, which suggests the early development of conversational patterns in which parents interrupt their high rate of vocalizing to listen to their infant when he or she vocalizes. Closer examination of longer chains of parent-infant vocal dialogues will provide more information about this apparent precursor to "conversation."

Infant movement, however, is a reliable modifier of parental smiling, looking more closely, and touching at all three time points during feeding (Table 3.7). Parental responsiveness to infant movement is highest at three months. Parental vocalizations show the same pattern at three weeks and three months but not in the newborn period, where there is little relationship between infant movement and parental vocal behavior (Table 3.7).

Again, the general pattern that we found for the feeding situation was evident in the play context as well. In summary, both mothers and fathers show a high degree of responsiveness to infant cues.

Parent Attitudes

Questionnaire data generally confirmed the pattern of behavioral results. The first factor, parental strain (resentment, disappointment, anxiety/worry) was lowest in the newborn period, increased to higher levels at the three week period, and then declined to an intermediate level by three months $F(2,72) = 7.69, p < .05$.

The pattern of parents' responses to these parental strain items over the three month period is a reasonable one: the least strain in the hospital context during the first days of infant life where the excitement and joy of the new infant is prevalent and where there is practical and social support from the pediatric nursing and medical staff; greater strain in the early period at home (three weeks) when the realities of a new infant in the family must be confronted; and a leveling off of parental strain by three months as the family adjusts to the infant. The infant exerts a great impact on the parents' life-style and finances, but the stress subsides as the parents' confidence in their parenting skills develops.

Of greatest relevance to the behavioral observations were two other factors. Regarding the second factor, the parents' attitudes about affectionate stimulation for the infant, there was a small difference between mothers and fathers at three days that favored fathers and an even smaller difference between mothers and fathers at three weeks that favored mothers, but by three months, mothers scored significantly higher than fathers on this affection and stimulation cluster of items, $F(2,72) = 10.43, p < .01$. Whereas mothers' scores were stable between the three day period and the three week period and increased between three weeks and three months, father scores declined between three days and three weeks and remained stable between three weeks and three months. Thus it appears that fathers' attitudes about affectionate stimulation of their infants during the first three months is most positive in the first days in the hospital, whereas mothers' attitudes in this regard are most positive during the third month. This is precisely the pattern of findings obtained for mothers' and fathers' behavior for the tactual-kinesthetic affectionate stimulation variable, "parent touches/moves part of baby."

Similar correspondence between patterns of parents' attitudes and behavior over time was observed for the behavior variable "parent shows infant toy to look at" and factor five that consisted of parental attributions of infant visual competence and the parents' intentions about use of toys in play with their infant. As would be expected, both mothers and fathers attributed greater visual competence to infants with increasing time and age of their infant, but a changing pattern of mother-father differences over time was obtained, $F(2,72) = 3.74$, $p < .05$. During the new born period in the hospital, fathers attributed greater visual competence to their infants than mothers. By three weeks, mothers attributed greater visual competence to their infants and did so at a level higher than fathers; between three weeks and three months both mothers' and fathers' attributions of infant visual competence increased, with mothers continuing to make greater attributions than fathers. A very similar pattern of mother-father differences and changes over time was found for the mothers' and fathers' visual stimulation behavior in the parent-infant interactions. For the variable "shows toy" fathers did so for more time than mothers at three days, but by three weeks mothers visually stimulated the infant with the toy more than the father and continued to do so during the three months observation. This parallel between shifts in parent attitudes about infants and their behavior in interaction with their infants suggests that parents' attitudes, including feelings about the baby, attributions about infant competence, and knowledge about "what's good for babies," may mediate the behavior observed in parent-infant interactions and their behavioral shifts across time.

IMPLICATIONS

The pattern of findings from our study suggests that mother and father play both similar and distinctive roles in early infancy. Parents of both sexes show a high degree of similarity both in terms of the types of behaviors that they direct toward their infants and their sensitivity and responsiveness to infant cues. The similarity in the patterns of behavior of mothers and fathers serves as a reminder that males and females should be viewed as parents as well as mothers and fathers. This similarity in mother-father behavior is consistent with our earlier studies (Parke, O'Leary, and West 1972; Parke and O'Leary 1976; Parke and Sawin 1975) as well as investigations conducted by others (Belsky, Chapter 5, this volume; Pedersen, Anderson and Cain, Chapter 4, this volume). The similarities in mother-father interaction patterns are probably due in part to both the capabilities and limitations of young infants that severely curtail the range of interactive behaviors and, at least in the case of our studies, the contextual restraints imposed by the use of structured interaction contexts.

However, there were mother-father differences, with mothers engaging in more routine caretaking (checks/changes diaper, dresses, grooms, covers) than fathers. Fathers, on the other hand, engaged in more social stimulation (mimicking the infant's facial expressions) than mothers—a possible precursor of father's emerging role as playmate (Clarke-Stewart, Chapter 6, this volume; Lamb, Chapter 2, this volume). This evidence of role differentiation was evident even as early as the newborn period and was still evident at three months. Although our focus is on the qualitative nature of early interaction, other evidence suggests that this role differentiation is reflected in the quantity of time that mothers and fathers devote to routine caretaking as well (Kotelchuck 1976; Rendina and Dickerscheid 1976; Richards et al. 1975). In spite of secular trends that are supporting new roles for mothers and fathers, a healthy dose of traditionalism in role allocations is still clearly in evidence. It is important, however, to recognize that the current patterns of father and mother roles are highly susceptible to secular trends, and one of our tasks is to monitor consistently these changes in father- (and mother-) infant interaction patterns. Eventually, we may be able to not only describe the changes but isolate the laws that govern the process of change in social interaction patterns (Parke 1976, 1979a).

The expression of affection distinguishes mothers and fathers as well. Mothers kiss babies more than fathers—or at least while being observed. In our earlier studies (Parke and O'Leary 1976), mothers smiled more at their newborns than fathers. These differences may reflect, in part, a more general sex difference, since females, whether mothers or not, appear to both express and react to affectional cues more than males (Maccoby and Jacklin 1974). Evidence that this male/female difference is evident in early infancy (Freedman 1974) suggests that biological factors as well as cultural expectations may play a role in accounting for these findings.

Another contributor to the mother-father differences is the sex of the infant. As in a wide range of other studies (Rebelsky and Hanks 1971; Rendina and Dickerscheid 1976), fathers and mothers—from the newborn period onward—treat boys and girls differently. Fathers generally show higher involvement with their sons, while mothers show the complementary pattern with heightened involvement with their daughter. In addition, some investigators report that fathers show more marked differences in their treatment (Lamb, Chapter 2, this volume) or their perceptions (Rubin, Provenzano, and Luria 1974) of boys and girls than mothers. Cross-cultural and comparative studies support these general trends. In a study of visiting patterns in Israeli kibbutzim, Gewirtz and Gewirtz (1968) found that fathers stayed for longer periods in the children's house with their four-month-old sons than with their infant daughters. West's and Konner's (1976) observations of male parental behavior among the Kung San

(Bushmen) reveal sex-of-infant differences. Although fathers interact more with male than female infants at both age levels studied (0 to 26 weeks and 27 to 99 weeks), the effect was significant only for the older infants. Other evidence of greater father-male infant interaction comes from Redican's (1976) long-term laboratory study of male-infant pairs—sex differences in contact were more pronounced than in adult female-infant pairs. Male adults had more extensive contact with male infants.

> Mothers tended to play with female infants whereas adult males did so with male infants. In general mothers interacted more positively with female infants and adult males with male infants. [Redican 1976, pp. 358-359].

The pattern of findings clearly indicate that the sex-typing process begins at a much earlier age than previously determined (compare Lynn 1974; Mischel 1970; Maccoby and Jacklin 1974 for reviews). The process may begin as early as the newborn period. In support of previous studies with older children (Goodenough 1957; Sears, Maccoby, and Levin 1957), recent observational studies suggest that fathers play a more intrusive and paramount role in the sex-typing process (Johnson 1963); fathers discriminate more than mothers in their treatment of male and female infants. In addition, boys are treated more discriminatively by their fathers than girls, which is consistent with other studies indicating that pressures toward sex-role adoption are stronger and occur at an earlier age for sons than daughters (Lansky 1967). Finally, father-absence studies (Herzog and Sudia 1973) underline the importance of the father's behavior in determining sex-role adoption in boys—especially in the early years (Stoltz 1954).

Although social learning explanations (compare Mischel 1970) can provide a framework for explaining the processes by which the differential socialization strategies of fathers and mothers develop, recent cross-cultural surveys suggest that caution must be exercised in generalizing the specific patterns observed in U. S. samples to other cultures. As West and Konner (1976) note, a variety of ecological, economic, and ideological variables must be considered in order to understand the particular sex-typing pressures in different cultures. It is clear that no single pattern can survive a cross-cultural comparison. Nor is it certain that the present picture will survive the next decade—in the light of the rapidly shifting sex-typing attitudes.

How generalizable are these findings to parent-infant interaction in the natural environment? All observations were made in a natural setting (either hospital or home), which should increase the generalizability of the results (Parke 1979b). But, the use of a structured situation may limit the generalizability, since these situations may have placed artificial restraints on the interaction and parents may have behaved differently in a nonstructured context.

However, "typical" or routine situations, such as feeding and play, were selected, and it is likely that these are situations that both parents experienced frequently in their daily interactions with their infant. Although mothers and fathers differ in their quantity of participation in feed and play situations, the difference is a relative one, and in the majority of families both parents contribute to these activities. Finally, the similarity of the pattern of our findings (concerning mother-father role differentiation and their differential treatment of boys and girls) to other investigations of parent-infant interaction, which have used unstructured observations in home settings, gives us greater confidence in our findings (Clarke-Stewart, Chapter 6, this volume; Kotelchuck 1976; Lamb, Chapter 2, this volume; Rendina and Dickerscheid 1976).

A final issue that merits comment is the issue of continuity of parent-infant interaction across the first three months of life. In general, there was little stability in the observed interaction patterns of parents and their infants from the newborn period to three months. A number of explanations for this general lack of continuity can be offered. First, the infant is undergoing rapid changes during the first three months of life in terms of motor and social repertoires. Second, the parents are acquiring increasing experience, which, in turn, may alter the qualitative aspects of parenting. Another type of explanation concerns the level of analyses. Continuity is often not found in analyses of behaviors such as looking, touching, moving and so on, which focus on discrete actions of a single individual. These measures fail to take into account the dyadic nature of the interaction; they focus on either the parent or infant alone rather than the parent-infant dyad. Possibly, measures that reflect the dyad rather than the individuals within the dyads may reveal more stability in social interaction. The development of a language for describing dyads (Hinde 1976), as well as larger units such as triads (Parke, Power, and Gottman 1979) is currently underway.

Continuity is, in fact, less likely to be found in discrete behaviors than in more molar assessments, which reflect stylistic characteristics of the interaction pattern (Cairns and Green 1979; Waters 1978). Focus on the degree of responsiveness or the sensitivity of the parents independently of the particular behaviors through which they demonstrate these qualities may reveal more continuity across time in parent-infant interaction patterns. However, it need not be assumed that this more molar level of analysis is incompatible with a more molecular level of analysis. One of the exciting challenges for current researchers is to demonstrate the ways various levels of analyses can be derived. Recent advances in statistical analyses of interactional data, such as sequential analyses (Gottman and Bakeman 1979) and time series (Gottman 1979), may permit a derivation of such constructs as "responsiveness" and "reciprocity" from an examination of the continuous interchanges between parent and infant. Assessments such as "parental responsiveness" can be derived from a sequential analysis of the ongoing interchanges between parent and infant by which responsiveness becomes defined as the proportion of times that parent reacts within some time period to an infant cue. Both the particular parent behaviors and infant elicitors may shift over time, but a content-free measure of responsiveness can still be derived.

One question that remains is how the definition of such contructs as "reciprocity" or "sensitivity" that are statistically derived matches the definition generated by raters, who use the full range of information available in an observation sample rather than restricting themselves to the moment-to-moment interchanges. By addressing more attention to both multiple levels of analyses and the ways in which these levels are derived, the issue of early continuity in parent-infant interaction may be better understood.

4

PARENT-INFANT AND HUSBAND-WIFE INTERACTIONS OBSERVED AT AGE 5 MONTHS

Frank A. Pedersen
Barbara J. Anderson
Richard L. Cain, Jr.

Over a decade ago Reubin Hill (1966) questioned psychologists' ability to conceive of the "family" in terms of other than the parent-child relationship, which at that time was synonymous with the mother-child dyad. The first step in considering the family as a group to be studied in its own right has been to recognize that fathers have roles in the family that extend beyond the provision of economic resources. Accordingly, studies have been reported in this volume and elsewhere that describe the characteristic behavior of fathers as the infant's caregiver, partner in play, and source of social and affectionate stimulation. Most often, the behaviors of fathers have been understood by making comparisons with mothers, establishing similarities and differences that are evident during interaction with their child. While this approach is a useful first step, much more is necessary to go beyond this strategy into the realm of considering the family as a complex interactive system.

In observing and describing maternal and paternal behavior, a dilemma arises as one attempts to identify an ecologically valid observational situation from which inferences may be made concerning the infant's larger experience in the family. A single observational situation defined by the investigator may

The authors gratefully acknowledge the constructive suggestions provided by Martha Zaslow. Appreciation is also expressed to Nancy Gist, who assisted in the enrollment of participants in the study as well as in other important ways, and Terry Pezza, who prepared an early version of the manuscript.

not be equally appropriate for the mother and the father. By controlling for the size of the social group in which observations are made while comparing parental gender, it is possible that the data may not generalize equally to both parents' typical experiences with the baby. Thus, a practice that seems as if it is well designed may introduce problems of ecological validity.

There has been little attention paid to the fact that different size groups involving the infant are differentially representative of fathers' and mothers' most characteristic times spent with an infant. From records kept by families in our study over a one-week period, we examined how much time was spent in all possible combinations of the three family members, father, mother, and five-month-old infant. We documented the simple but important point that, for families where the father was the principal wage earner, the most characteristic social group involving the infant for the mother was a two-person unit, the mother and infant without the father being present. By far, the most character-istic social unit involving the infant for the father was the three-person group of mother, father, and infant. Time in which the father and baby were together without the mother being a part of the situation did occur, to be sure, but it averaged only about one-half hour per day. One of our research goals, therefore, was to compare maternal and paternal behavior in similar size social groups as well as different size groups, which nonetheless may be more representative of each's experiences in the family.

Changes in the stimulus characteristics of different social groups have been called "second-order" effects by Bronfenbrenner (1974a), recognizing that the presence of one person may alter the interaction between the other two mem-bers. In research on this problem to date, some inconsistencies have been found. In observations during the newborn period conducted in the hospital setting (Parke and O'Leary 1976), the presence of both parents seemed to enhance aspects of parent-infant interaction. Fathers were found to exhibit more nurtur-ant behavior than the mother in a three-person setting, but they showed an amount equal to the mother when alone with the baby. Moreover, both mother and father smiled more at the baby when the spouse was present than absent. In contrast, studies at older ages in the laboratory or home (Lamb, Chapter 2, this volume; Clarke-Stewart, Chapter 6, this volume) have found decrements in behavior rates for both parent and child in three-person groups compared to two-person groups. Comparison of these results is difficult because the studies differed in both the setting and the ages of the children. Our observations with relatively young infants in the home setting will add additional data that may help to establish the boundaries of these findings.

While changes in rates of parental behavior are expected in different size groups, an interesting question arises as to how readily the infant accommodates to such change. Previous research on infant responsiveness to varying rates of interaction have been done primarily in dyadic contexts (Brazelton et al. 1975; Yogman et al. 1976). Results show that infants alter their behavior appropriately in response to varying activity with their social partner, either mother or father. If changes in interaction rates that occur in three-person groups are more complex than in dyadic settings, the young infant may be unable to monitor its own behavior and respond appropriately to the subtle cues of variation in the level of adult activity. This question is important because it bears on whether there is a good "fit" between interactive partners in the setting in which much father-infant interaction occurs.

Finally, considering experiences in the three-person setting brings into focus the other dyadic relationship in the family, the husband and wife. An important question that has received only slight attention is whether characteristics of the spouse relationship influence parent-infant interaction. Theoretical development of this possibility has been particularly deficient. Bowlby (1969) conceived of the husband/father role as a "constant" in different families, that of providing emotional and material support to the mother and thereby enhancing the mother-infant relationship. Clearly, strategies are needed to analyze effects of variation in the husband-wife relationship. One way in which the interplay of the spouse unit and parent-infant interaction may be analyzed is by examining the interdependencies among the different family dyads within a single situational context. Clarifying some of the linkages between spouse interaction and behavior directed toward the baby within the same situation will aid our understanding of ways in which a three-person group of mother, father, and infant is different in content and dynamics than a dyadic unit of parent and infant. Bringing into focus the spouse relationship and its possible mediating effects on the amount and type of behavior directed toward the baby will contribute toward our fundamental goal of understanding early experience in a family setting.

In summary, this investigation attempts to add an ecological perspective to research on fathers and infants by drawing attention to some of the features of interaction that occur by virtue of parental specialization in child care and work roles. Parent-infant interaction will be compared in similar and different social groups, and special attention will be given to spouse interaction and its possible mediating influence on each parent's behavior with the baby.

METHODOLOGY

Sample

The participants in the investigation were 41 middle-income, Caucasian families with a firstborn, five-month-old infant. There were 23 families with male infants and 18 with female infants. The parents were volunteers recruited through childbirth preparation groups during 1976, and all families resided in the Washington, D.C. metropolitan area. The mean age was 29 years for the mothers and 31 years for the fathers, and the couples had been married an average of 4.6 years. The mean educational level for mothers was 16.1 years, and the mean for fathers was 17.3 years. In each family the pregnancy had been uncomplicated, and at age five months, all infants were reported to be healthy and developing normally. Most mothers provided the primary care for their infants, but there were seven families in which the mother worked full-time outside of the home.

Observation Methodology

The observation methodology was designed to provide simultaneous time-sampled descriptions of interaction among the three possible dyadic units in a three-person family: mother and infant, father and infant, and husband and wife. The time-sampling cycle was a 10-second observing period followed by a 20-second recording period, repeated throughout the observation.

Parental behavior categories were selected on the basis of theoretical considerations or previous empirical findings relevant to three issues: (1) behaviors associated with some developmental outcomes in the child, (2) behaviors in which parental role specialization has been suggested, and (3) behaviors that might occur differentially with either male or female infants.

Following the pilot stages of the investigation, 18 categories were utilized. Of these, 6 were rejected for the final analyses, primarily because of relatively low frequency of occurrence (observed in less than 1 percent of the time units), which was also associated with less adequate observer reliability. The eight remaining categories of parental behavior are: mutual visual regard; verbalizations; vocalizations; smiling to the infant; providing various kinds of physical contact such as holding, rocking or cuddling, touching, and vigorous tactile-kinesthetic stimulation; focused social play; play involving inanimate objects; and feeding either liquids or solids to the infant.

Infant behaviors sampled were similar to other investigations at this developmental stage (Yarrow, Rubenstein, and Pedersen 1975) and included the baby's visual focus on the mother's or father's face, positive vocalizations, smiling, fussing or crying (a low frequency event in this investigation and therefore omitted from the analyses), and exploratory behavior with objects.

Spouse interactions were coded when all three people were together. Categories included general verbal exchanges, verbal exchanges regarding the infant, requesting or providing help in the care of the infant, and expressions of positive and negative effect. Our interest in utilizing observational measures of husband-wife interaction was to provide an alternative to traditional global indexes of "marital satisfaction" and other self-report techniques that are highly subject to response sets and social desirability motives (Wills, Weis, and Patterson

1974). Moreover, observational measures permit more detailed analyses of the interdependencies among the marital and parent-infant dyads.

Three observers, each visiting comparable numbers of families, collected all of the data. Interobserver agreement was achieved through intensive participation in the code development phase and the observation of ten families by pairs of observers before and during the data collection period. Periodic reviews of videotaped family interactions were done during the data collection period to ensure adherence to category definitions. Reliability of all behavior categories ranges from .70 to .99, based on product-moment correlations between pairs of observers utilizing frequency scores derived in identical fashion to those used in the data analyses.

Structure and Schedule of Observations

Four visits were made to each home around the time the infant was five months old. The purpose of the first visit was to explain the investigation in detail, secure informed consent, obtain background demographic information, and encourage the parents to feel at ease with the observer. Subsequently, two one-hour home observations were made about a week apart. These visits were conducted during a period when both parents were typically home and the infant was expected to be awake, most often during the early part of the evening. We emphasized to the parents that our interest was in the baby's "typical" experiences during this period. No constraints were made upon the parents to stay in the same room, engage the infant in prescribed ways, or avoid certain behavior or activities. The fourth visit was a 90-minute observation of the mother and infant when the father was out of the home. This mother-infant observation was typically conducted sometime between the two evening observations.

RESULTS AND DISCUSSION

For all of the analyses that we will report, separate comparisons were first made for male and female infants. We found no main effects for sex of infant. Moreover, considering the total number of comparisons made, there were fewer interactions than would be expected by chance with other variables involving sex of the infant. Therefore, male and female infants were combined for all of the analyses. The absence of statistical interactions associated with sex of the child may appear discordant with the emphasis on such findings in other chapters. We speculate that there are two explanations for this difference. First, from Lamb's data (Chapter 2), it appears that the degree of influence of infant gender is more prominent in the second year of life than it is in the first. Second, it is possible

TABLE 4.1

Comparisons of Maternal and Paternal Behaviors Directed to Infant in Two-Person and Three-Person Groups

Variable	Two-Person Groups		Three-Person Groups		F Ratios		
	Mothers	Fathers	Mothers	Fathers	Sex of Parent	Size of Group	Interaction
Mutual visual regard	.18	.15	.08	.06	0.7	23.6^a	0.1
Verbalizations	.49	.41	.25	.18	6.5^b	98.2^a	0.3
Vocalizations	.12	.16	.07	.06	0.9	18.2^a	2.6
Smiles	.13	.09	.07	.04	4.9^b	14.9^b	0.3
Hold, move, or support	.33	.34	.20	.19	0.0	26.3^a	0.1
Rock or cuddle	.04	.03	.02	.02	0.5	5.5^b	0.1
Vigorous tactile-kinesthetic stimulation	.01	.03	.01	.02	2.5	1.3	0.3
Touch	.09	.10	.06	.06	0.0	8.6^a	0.5
Focused social play	.05	.06	.02	.03	0.4	11.6^a	0.0
Play with objects	.07	.07	.03	.03	0.0	14.0^a	0.2
Feed liquids	.10	.03	.06	.03	6.3^b	1.8	2.4
Feed solids	.06	.05	.06	.04	0.4	0.2	0.0

[a] $p < .01$.
[b] $p < .05$.

Note: Entries represent the mean proportion of observational intervals in which a behavior occurred; $df = 1,40$ for all comparisons.
Source: Compiled by the authors.

that the parents in this investigation were more committed, consciously or implicitly, to "androgynous parenting" than the parents in other samples. This possibility is suggested by our recruitment of research participants through child-birth preparation groups, an experience that may have been selectively attractive to parents with less traditional sex-typing behaviors.

The findings presented first are comparisons of maternal and paternal behaviors derived from the two visits when all three family members were home. Because parents were encouraged to go about their usual activities, sometimes the mother or the father or even both left the room where the baby was for short intervals. In addition, one parent occasionally took the infant to another room, leaving the other parent out of the situation. Consequently there were naturally occurring transitions between two-person and three-person groups, which changed depending upon family activities and the needs of different individuals. For approximately 70 percent of the observation intervals, all three people were together in the same room. The remaining intervals provided adequate information to compare the effect of the size of the group on both mother-infant and father-infant interactions. It is important to point out that these were naturally occurring changes in group structure. If we had asked that one parent leave the situation, certainly the other parent would have felt under considerably greater scrutiny by the observers.

Table 4.1 provides a comparison of mothers and fathers interacting with the infant in two-person and three-person groups. All frequency scores are expressed as proportions of the number of time units that a particular group was observed. Separate analyses of variance were performed for each of the 12 measures. Three of the twelve variables show a significant overall difference for mothers and fathers: verbalizations directed to the baby, smiling, and feeding liquids. Similar results for two of the three differences are found in other investigations, while one is more problematic; a higher rate of maternal smiling, as compared to paternal smiling, appears consistently in virtually all of the investigations that included the variable (Parke, O'Leary, and West 1972; Parke and O'Leary 1976; Field 1978). That the mothers in this sample fed liquids significantly more than did the fathers is consistent with the preponderance of investigations that have found mothers assuming more caregiving functions (see Lamb, Parke and Sawin, Belsky, and Clarke-Stewart, this volume). One should note, however, that this investigation included a high proportion of breast-fed infants (88 percent), and that fact is surely the most simple explanation for these findings. Our finding of a higher rate of maternal verbalizations is consistent with Rebelsky and Hanks (1971) and the findings and interpretative emphasis that Clarke-Stewart (Chapter 6, this volume) places on this variable, but other results are discordant (Parke and Sawin, Belsky, this volume; Field 1978).

There were several variables for which other research would lead to expectations of differences between mothers and fathers, but, in fact, we found none. First, mothers and fathers did not differ significantly in rates of vocalizations,

TABLE 4.2

Comparison of Infant Behaviors in Two-Person and Three-Person Groups

Variable	Two-Person Groups		Three-Person Groups		F Ratios		
	To Mother	To Father	To Mother	To Father	Sex of Parent	Size of Group	Interaction
Socially directed behavior							
Look at face	.210	.210	.109	.102	.0	27.1[a]	0.4
Directed smiling and laughing	.037	.032	.015	.015	.1	7.9[a]	1.3
Directed positive vocalization	.066	.078	.027	.020	.1	20.0[a]	0.4
Behavior toward inanimate environment							
Attend object	.223		.175	.175	n. a.	6.5[b]	n. a.
Manipulate object	.208		.175	.175	n. a.	2.1	n. a.
Vocalization during exploration	.062		.044		n. a.	4.8[b]	n. a.

n. a.: not applicable.
[a] $p < .01$
[b] $p < .05$.

Note: Entries represent the mean proportion of observational intervals in which a behavior occurred; $df = 1,40$ for all comparisons.

Source: Compiled by the authors.

that is, high-pitched, often imitative sounds, and ways of speaking very uncharacteristic of adult-to-adult conversation. This style of "baby talk" has been identified by Ferguson (1964) as characteristic of mothers in six cultures; in the present sample, speaking this way was equally characteristic of mothers and fathers, as Field (1978) found for mothers and primary-caregiver fathers. Second, we found no significant difference between parents in the rate of vigorous tactile-kinesthetic stimulation, a style of interaction especially emphasized by Lamb (Chapter 2, this volume) and Clarke-Stewart (Chapter 6, this volume) as characteristic of fathers with older-age children. Finally, both object-mediated play and focused social play occurred with equal frequency for mothers and fathers; play has sometimes been considered the hallmark of paternal interaction. We interpret these "nonfindings" as providing some qualification to an emphasis on differences between mothers and fathers. They provide support for the view that fathers have considerable role flexibility, a point emphasized by Pedersen and Robson (1969) and Russell (1978).

In contrast to the sparseness of overall behavioral differences between mothers and fathers, the size of the group in which interaction occurred had a very strong impact on parental behavior. Table 4.1 indicates that 9 out of 12 parental measures are significantly different for the two settings, with higher frequencies of behavior consistently demonstrated in two-person groups. Moreover, the same effects are seen for the behaviors of both mothers and fathers. A similar effect of size of the group on parental verbalizations (Lamb, Chapter 2, this volume) and other behaviors for mothers (Clarke-Stewart, Chapter 6, this volume) has been described, but our findings show broad effects for both parents. The enhancement of positive effect described when the spouse is present during interaction with newborns in the hospital setting (Parke and O'Leary 1976) did not occur with five-month-old infants in the home. Perhaps there are differences in affective responsiveness during the earliest days of parenthood, especially in the hospital environment.

When we examined infant behaviors involving either parent across two-person and three-person groups, precisely comparable results occurred. Table 4.2 shows that there was a significant increase in the rates of three measures of directed social behavior in the two-person groups. The infant's looking at either parent's face as well as smiling and vocalizing while simultaneously looking at the parent were all significantly higher in two-person groups. Clearly, the young infant does accommodate to changes in activity in different size groups, and this was true whether the dyadic social partner was mother or father.

When one examines the means in the two settings, it is clear that the infant did not change its overall rate of behavior as much as it changed the distribution of behavior. The mean for behavior toward either parent in a two-person setting was almost equivalent to the sum of the means for behavior toward each parent in the three-person setting. This results, however, in a decrease in interaction with either parent in the three-person setting as compared to the dyadic setting. Moreover, two out of three measures of infant behavior directed toward the inanimate environment (visually attending to objects and vocalizing while exploring objects) were higher in two-person settings. This suggests that more information processing with inanimate objects occurred in the two-person groups. Undoubtedly, some of this increase occurred in association with toy-mediated play, which was more prevalent in two-person settings.

The importance of these findings goes beyond pointing out that the impact of social context is greater than that of parental gender on parent and infant behavior. Rather, these results emphasize the importance of the social context or size of social group, which is ecologically representative of each parent's behavior in the family. In families where the father has the primary wage-earner role, more of his interactions with the infant occur in three-person settings, while the mother in families with such role organization spends relatively more time with the infant in two-person settings. As a consequence, the infant often has dramatically different experiences with each parent. These differences were highlighted by comparing the father's behavior in three-person groups with the sample of the mother's behavior obtained during the 90-minute observation in the daytime when the father was not home. For every variable but one (vigorous tactile-kinesthetic stimulation), the mothers were significantly higher than the fathers. These results were so straightforward that they are not presented in detail.

It must be remembered that previous analysis confounds gender of parent and size of social group. This comparison represents the ecological reality that occurs with a traditional division between father and mother of wage-earner and child care roles, respectively. The analyses in Tables 4.1 and 4.2 indicate, however, that differences are due more to the influence of the social group in which interaction occurs than to inherent differences between mothers and fathers that cut across all social settings. One implication of these findings is that alternative divisions of work roles may have a profound effect on promoting more similar relationships for mother and father with the infant. Our data suggest that more intense interaction between father and infant might not occur simply by spending more time in the home; rather, more intensive interaction is likely when the father spends time with the infant when the mother is not also present.

These analyses, which point to the importance of social group size in studying mothers, fathers, and infants, bring into focus for the three-person setting the third dyad in the family, the husband and wife. In none of the previous observational investigations of early experience has there been an explicit recognition that this relationship might bear on the infant's experiences. Our interest was to gain further understanding of the psychological processes that influence behavior in the three-person setting. By focusing upon the moment-to-moment variation among the three dyads, we attempted to elucidate linkages between spouse exchanges and parent-infant interactions in the same situational context. We asked whether spouse interaction has a mediating effect on the amount or type of behavior directed toward the baby, or conversely, if interaction with the infant has a controlling influence on spouse interaction. It is questions of this nature that expand consideration of the parent-infant relationships into a study of the family as an interactive system.

The data for these analyses consist of a subset of the data summarized in Table 4.1, the intervals when the three family members were together in the same room. First, 51 percent of these units included some husband-wife communication. This is an important descriptive finding because it indicates that husband-wife interaction has a high frequency of occurrence, even though previously it had been considered largely irrelevant to the infant's experiences. To establish if there was any synchrony between husband-wife interaction and behavior directed toward the baby, we initially partitioned the data according to presence or absence of any spouse communication within each ten-second observation interval. We then compared the rates of behavior directed toward the infant during units when the parents were communicating with each other with rates during intervals when the parents were not. This was carried out separately for mothers and fathers. These results appear in Table 4.3.

Since these analyses are based on a major subset of the evening observations, times when mother, father, and infant were together in the same room, the variables that previously showed a main effect for parental gender, verbalizations, smiling, and feeding liquids also significantly discriminated mothers and fathers in this analysis. In addition, when all three family members were together, vigorous tactile-kinesthetic stimulation was significantly higher for fathers than mothers. This finding did not emerge in the analyses summarized in Table 4.1. Apparently, data from observations of two-person groups introduced enough additional error variance to dilute a finding that we see in the data for the three-person situation alone. This finding brings our results into line with those reported by Lamb (Chapter 2, this volume), who found similar robust handling of infants and toddlers by fathers with data based principally on three-person situations. We also see this parental gender difference, but only in the three-person situation. Thus, it appears that the three-person situation lends itself to somewhat greater role specialization.

Of greater import for the question of spouse interaction and the parent-infant relationship, the data show that for nine out of twelve variables the spouse communication condition was significantly associated with rates of behavior directed toward the infant. It appears that behaviors that require greater focused attention on the part of the parent—making eye contact, talking, smiling, and playing in various ways with the baby—are inhibited when there is active spouse communication. These behaviors emerge more strongly in time intervals when there is no communication between parents. Behaviors that require less focused attention, such as holding the baby, rocking or cuddling, and feeding solids, are not affected by whether the parents are communicating with each other. There was one exception to this overall pattern: feeding liquids was more prevalent during periods when husband and wife interacted with each

TABLE 4.3

Comparisons of Maternal and Paternal Behaviors Directed to Infant During Intervals in Which Spouse Communication Did or Did Not Occur

	Intervals in Which Spouse Communication Occurred		Intervals in Which No Spouse Communication Occurred		F Ratios		
	Mothers	Fathers	Mothers	Fathers	Sex of Parent	Spouse Communication Condition	Interaction
Mutual visual regard	.05	.05	.11	.08	1.2	54.1^a	3.9
Verbalizations	.17	.15	.34	.24	9.2^a	100.8^a	13.3^a
Vocalizations	.04	.04	.10	.09	0.2	43.7^a	0.6
Smiles	.04	.03	.10	.06	8.5^a	48.8^a	3.6
Hold, move, or support	.19	.20	.20	.18	0.0	0.8	2.2
Rock and cuddle	.02	.02	.02	.01	0.6	0.4	2.7
Vigorous tactile-kinesthetic stimulation	.00	.01	.01	.02	5.6^b	13.9^a	1.2
Touch	.05	.06	.07	.06	0.0	6.7^a	0.8
Focused social play	.01	.02	.04	.04	1.2	33.4^a	0.6
Play with objects	.02	.02	.04	.03	0.9	19.5^a	5.1^b
Feed liquids	.07	.04	.06	.02	5.0^b	6.7^a	1.2
Feed solids	.05	.05	.06	.04	0.3	0.1	0.5

[a] $p < .01$.
[b] $p < .05$.
Note: Entries represent the mean proportion of observation intervals in which a behavior occurred; $df = 1,40$ for all comparisons.
Source: Compiled by the authors.

other. Perhaps nursing or giving a bottle quiets the activity of the baby directed toward the external environment in such a way that the parents are drawn together to talk during these periods. Alternately, parents who have many things to talk about may "save" them until a good time to talk, such as the feeding period.

There were also two significant interactions of parental gender and the spouse communication condition: verbalizations directed toward the infant and play that involved directing the baby's attention to toys. Rates for both of these behaviors increased significantly more for mothers than fathers when there was no ongoing spouse communication. Our findings suggest that, in synchronizing infant and spouse interactions, in some ways the mothers and infants in our sample were drawn together a bit more strongly than were the fathers and infants.

One additional set of analyses was performed—a comparison of the infant's behavior to each parent in relation to the occurrence of communication between the parents. These analyses appear in Table 4.4. The data show that all three measures of the infant's social behavior are extraordinarily well coordinated with the changes in parental behavior. During periods of no spouse communication, when focused social interactions with the infant increase, the infant also shows increased rates of socially directed behaviors to both mother and father. There was also a significant interaction of gender of parent by spouse communication on the infant looking at the parent's face. The rate of change in looking toward mothers was greater than looking toward fathers, a finding that most likely parallels the statistical interaction associated with maternal verbalizations. These results go beyond the findings reported in Table 4.2, which merely show an accommodation to the difference between one or two social partners. In fact, the infant at only five months of age shows the ability to engage in a complex intermeshing of behavior with both parents that is also coordinated with their behavior to each other. This suggests that the three-person group, which typically the presence of the father creates, may provide unique learning opportunities for the infant and may contribute to its expanded repertoire of behavior.

Viewing these findings together, they explain many of the psychological processes associated with the second-order effect. They also provide ideas regarding certain "blends" of behavior, which are responsive to the needs of various family members in the three-person situation. In a family with a traditional role organization, some mothers may desire an opportunity for adult interaction after extensive periods of providing child care and performing household tasks; alternatively, fathers may also wish to discuss their personal concerns. One solution to these needs might be to coordinate spouse interaction periods with the infant's feeding, a combination of activities that mixes readily. If one parent desires to engage in more autonomous activities or perform household tasks that must be done that require considerable attention, the other parent might find that these are periods well suited for more focused interaction with the baby. In either case, they are not periods so readily coordinated with

TABLE 4.4

Comparisons of Infant Behaviors During Intervals in Which Spouse Communication Did or Did Not Occur

	Intervals in Which Spouse Communication Occurred		Intervals in Which No Spouse Communication Occured		F Ratios		
	To Mother	To Father	To Mother	To Father	Sex of Parent	Spouse Communication Condition	Interaction
Socially directed behavior							
Look at face	.08	.09	.13	.12	0.18	31.80[a]	3.93[b]
Directed smile or laughter	.01	.01	.02	.03	0.28	20.10[a]	0.34
Directed positive vocalization	.02	.01	.04	.03	1.5	16.00[a]	0.05
Behavior toward inanimate environment							
Attend object	.17	.17	.18	.18	n. a.	0.14	n. a.
Manipulate object	.18	.18	.17	.17	n. a.	0.32	n. a.
Vocalization during exploration	.06	.06	.05	.05	n. a.	7.52[a]	n. a.

n. a.: not applicable.

[a] $p < .01$.

[b] $p < .05$.

Note: Entries represent the proportion of observation intervals in which a behavior occurred; $df = 1,40$ for all comparisons.

Source: Compiled by the authors.

spouse interaction, and attempting such exchanges is likely to introduce competing needs for attention. Another alternative is to recognize that "turn-taking" is possible in directing attention to baby or spouse, and thus the needs of each family member for social interaction can be made without placing one in a competitive position relative to another. Of course, different intersections of needs and expectations are likely to occur with, for example, different parental role organizations, developmental levels, or temperamental characteristics of the infant as well as other idiosyncratic factors. By establishing linkages between the spouse relationship and parent-infant interaction, we are suggesting that it may be possible to identify ways in which husband and wife either support or perhaps conflict with each other's parental and marital roles.

CONCLUSIONS

In examining behaviors that are relatively intrinsic to mothers and fathers, that is, behaviors that consistently discriminate parents across different social contexts or groups, we are impressed more by similarities than differences. The mothers in our sample spoke to their babies, smiled, and, as a consequence of breast feeding, fed liquids more frequently than did fathers. Behaviors that previous investigations identified as especially characteristic of interaction for one gender of parent or another (such as distinctive speech styles, robust physical handling of the infant, and social or toy-mediated play) were engaged in equally by mothers and fathers when interactions were appraised across two-person and three-person groups.

Largely as a consequence of parental specialization in the wage-earner and child care roles, there are important differences in the social groups in which mothers and fathers more often interact with the infant. Our data show clearly that parent and infant allocate behaviors to each other differentially, based on the size of the social group. In the three-person situation, there is a decrease in rates of either maternal or paternal interaction with the infant. But rates of both parents summed together closely approximate the overall amount of interaction the infant experiences in the dyadic setting with either parent. In complementary fashion, size of social group has a very similar effect on infant behavior.

Changes in each parent's behavior in the three-person setting also occur as a function of spouse interaction. Moreover, changes are selective. There is a decrement in those responses that demand more focused attention and would seem to preclude simultaneous interaction between parent-infant and husband-wife dyads. Behaviors such as smiling, vocalizing, and directing visual attention to the baby, as well as vigorous handling and play, are less likely to occur when there is ongoing spouse interaction. Other responses such as feeding solids, holding, or rocking the baby are not inhibited in the presence of ongoing spouse communication. Feeding liquids, on the other hand, often occurs concurrently with spouse interaction. More than simply the amount of behavior changes when all family members are together; it is clear there is a complex orchestration of amount and type of interaction dependent on the parent's entry into exchanges with the spouse. The five-month-old infant appears sensitive and responsive to these changes and alters its behavior in relation to changes in activity with both mother and father.

In our sample the three-person situation was most representative of the father's interaction time with the infant. Yet, increasingly families are creating new work role division strategies. In some families the three-person situation is becoming more representative of the mother's interaction time. In other families, a shift away from traditional work roles results in an increase in the amount of time the father spends with the infant in dyadic situations.

Our findings emphasize the importance of being sensitive to the size of the social group that is most ecologically valid for each parent in a particular family. Moreover, our data document that knowledge about the interactional processes involving husband and wife contributes to understanding the kind and amount of stimulation parents are likely to provide the infant in three-person settings. Understanding of the infant's early environment has been enhanced by the inclusion of fathers as a source of experience. To the accumulation of new information on this problem, our findings bring an ecological perspective and point to an additional, remarkably complex synchronization between the parents' interactions with each other and with their young infants.

5

A FAMILY ANALYSIS OF PARENTAL INFLUENCE ON INFANT EXPLORATORY COMPETENCE

Jay Belsky

The inclusion of the father in the study of early experience does more than simply turn the mother-infant dyad into the mother-father-infant triad. What it does is transform a two-person relationship into a family system. From a theoretical standpoint, separate examinations of the mother-infant and father-infant relationships are incomplete characterizations of the infant's early experience within the family. A more complete picture of such experience must evidence awareness that not only do parents interact with one another but that they together, as a family unit, exert an influence upon the young child.

With respect to the issue of interaction between parents, we have witnessed in recent years a growing appreciation by developmental psychologists of the significance of the spousal relationship for the developing infant (Lerner and Spanier 1978). The work of Pedersen and his colleagues is especially noteworthy in this regard. In documenting the relationship between maternal feeding competence and the emotional tenor of the spousal relationship (Pedersen 1975), as well as that between second-order effects (that is, reductions in parental activity associated with spousal presence) and levels of husband-wife interaction (Pedersen, Anderson, and Cain, Chapter 4, this volume), these investigators have not only shed light upon the processes whereby the spousal relationship impinges upon the infant but, in so doing, have stimulated others to pursue this fascinating area of inquiry (for example, Belsky, In press [a]; Price 1977).

The research reported in this chapter was conducted as part of the author's doctoral dissertation. Appreciation is expressed to Dr. Henry N. Ricciuti for the support and guidance he provided throughout this project.

A second issue, the joint or combined impact of mother and father upon infant development, has received much less empirical attention. In fact, the large majority of research on the role of father during infancy has been surprisingly conservative in its emphasis; investigators have been content to identify similarities and differences between the mother-infant and father-infant relationships by repeating with fathers investigatory procedures that have been previously employed with mothers (see Feldman and Ingham 1973; Kotelchuck et al. 1975; Willemsen et al. 1974, in the area of attachment; and Yogman et al. 1976; Field 1978, in the area of face-to-face interaction). Only Clarke-Stewart's (Chapter 6, this volume) small-sample longitudinal study of mother-father-infant interaction, with its concern for the developmental correlates of differences between parents, is a notable exception to this rule. Interestingly, much more work of this type has been carried out on families with older children (Bronson 1966; Hoffman 1960; Honzik 1967; Wyer 1965). Bronfenbrenner's (1961b) early work on adolescent development, for example, illustrates the potential of a more comprehensive analysis of parenting. In this investigation of the antecedents of responsibility and leadership, he noted that the authority exercised by a single parent was much less predictive of development among tenth graders than was the relative authority of both parents considered together.

In the light of these few suggestive findings, and the general absence of data concerning the combined impact of mother and father upon infant development, the purposes of this chapter are twofold: (1) to extend the comparative work on mothering and fathering during infancy by examining the differential influence of mother and father on the exploratory competence of their 15-month-old child and, more significantly, (2) to expand the scope of our thinking regarding parental influence during infancy by examining the joint impact of parents on the development of their infant's competence. In moving beyond the interesting, yet conservative comparative analysis of mothering and fathering during infancy, the guiding theme of the present work is that a family analysis of parental influence will expand our understanding of early experience more than will individual and separate examinations of mothering and fathering.

Before describing the present investigation, some comments are in order regarding the procedures employed to assess infant competence. A decision was made to forgo the use of standard infant tests, based upon two considerations: the repeated demonstrations that standard tests in the infancy period are of limited predictive utility (for review see Lewis 1976) and the view that most testing procedures place questionable constraints upon the behavior of young children (compare Ginsburg and Koslowski 1976). These considerations, along with the emerging consensus that accurate and meaningful appraisals of children's competence will emerge from careful observations of their everyday interactions in natural life settings (Carew, Chan, and Halfar 1975; Charlesworth 1975; Spiker 1977), served as impetus for the development of a naturalistic procedure for assessing the quality of infants' exploratory behavior as well as their motivation to explore.

The decision to focus upon play and exploratory behavior* as criteria of competence was influenced by the work of a variety of investigators pursuing distinct, though often interrelated, concerns. One body of evidence has highlighted the need for systematic observations of what it is that infants do while exploring (Haith and Campos 1977; Weissler and McCall 1976)—in order to complement the mass of data that has been accumulated concerning the characteristics of stimuli that make them attractive for exploration (for example, the novel, the complex, the discrepant). In addition, a second and more recent body of literature has indicated that, since the quality of infants' exploratory pursuits is sensitive to ontogenetic transitions (Fein and Apfel 1976; Fenson et al. 1976; Inhelder et al. 1972; Lowe 1975; McCall 1974), careful analysis of exploration and play might provide information relevant to early competence.

In drawing upon both of these literatures and, in addition, the recent writings of Yarrow concerning mastery motivation in infancy (Yarrow 1976; Yarrow and Pedersen 1976; Yarrow et al. 1978), exploratory competence was conceptualized in terms of both the motivation to explore and the skills displayed while exploring. Operationally this meant paying careful attention to the amount of time infants spent playing with a set of toys made available to them and the nature of their manipulative activities. Though no attempt was made to obtain external validation of the measures utilized, the competent explorer was hypothesized to play with toys for extended rather than fleeting periods of time and exploit their unique properties (for example, placing a peg within a hole, dialing a toy phone). In developing methods and procedures, the present work drew heavily upon that of Robert McCall (1974).

To summarize, the purpose of the present investigation was to examine the differential and combined impact of mother and father on infant development. This was to be done by establishing relations between patterns of parental behavior and exploratory competence displayed by 15-month-olds while playing with a set of standard toys in their own homes. It should be noted that the evidence to be presented is only suggestive in regard to the issue of cause and effect (that is, data on infant competence and parental behavior were gathered at the same time). Despite this limitation, the language of influence, particularly that of parents affecting infant development, will be employed for heuristic purposes. The intent is not to deny the possibility that infant competence influences parental behavior (compare Bell 1968; Clarke-Stewart, Chapter 6, this volume; Lewis and Rosenblum 1974) or to minimize the limits of conclusions drawn

---

*In line with Weissler and McCall (1976), play and exploration are considered indistinguishable as they occur in the child's ecologically valid, ongoing stream of behavior.

from contemporaneous correlational data, but, rather, it is to highlight the potential richness of a family analysis of mothering and fathering during infancy.

METHODS

Sample

Forty middle class* families with infants 15 months of age were recruited between April and July 1978 from the Ithaca and Cortland, New York areas to participate in the research by means of an introductory letter and follow-up phone call (58 percent acceptance). Families who agreed to participate were traditional in terms of household division of labor—that is, the fathers left home each day to go to work and the mothers remained home to serve as the infant's primary caregiver. In 24 households the infants were male and in 16 they were female; 18 were first-borns and 22 were later-borns. The occupations of fathers participating in the study varied greatly and included salesman, small business-man, doctor, lawyer, elementary and high school teacher, and graduate student. As only a limited percentage of families (19 percent) enrolled in the study were affiliated with a college or university, the sample is considered representative of middle class, two-parent families in upstate New York.

Observations

Families were observed on two separate weekdays, for two hours each day, at a time that would maximize the likelihood of observing three naturally occur-ring social situations: mother alone with child, father alone with child, and both parents together with child. Within a week of the second observation of family interaction, infant exploratory competence was assessed.

The selection of observation time was guided by a desire to sample seg-ments of the day representative of the young child's experience with each parent. Since infants in the study families spent the preponderance of their waking hours with mother and were primarily available to their fathers in late afternoon and early evening after work hours, observations were usually sched-uled at this time. Observations typically began one hour before the father arrived home (to see mother alone with child) and continued for an additional hour following his arrival.

---

*In the present investigation, middle class was defined as both parents having had some college experience or one parent having graduated from college.

In selecting this time of day to observe the family, it was recognized that the parents would be differentially familiar to their infants. Mothers were seen after they had spent an entire day with the child, whereas fathers were observed at a time when they were both relatively novel to the child and fresh in the parenting role. Despite this very real psychological difference,* this period was selected because it was considered to reflect the family members' everyday experiences with each other.

Prior to beginning each observation, and during an initial visit to each home that preceded formal data collection, parents were encouraged to go about their regular household routines and ignore the observer's presence while he followed the baby. The primary purpose of this visit, in addition to describing in more detail the nature of the study ("to learn about the infant's everyday world") and scheduling the later home visits, was to establish rapport between the observer and the parents. It was felt that visiting both parents in a friendly fashion before data collection was begun would minimize parental self-consciousness and needs to display socially desirable behavior.

During the observations, 15 parent, 8 infant, and 5 spousal behaviors were recorded by means of a precoded checklist employed on a time sampling basis; only parental behaviors (13 of the 15) are considered in this report. Time intervals were established by means of an inconspicuous earphone attached to a portable cassette recorder (compare Clarke-Stewart 1973), and behavior was observed and recorded during alternating 15-second periods. That is, when a behavior was observed within a 15-second "observe" period, an entry was made on the checklist during the following 15-second "record" period. Throughout the two hour period, then, one hour of observation was obtained. This schedule was employed because of the large number of behaviors being coded and the intensity of triadic interaction.

The 13 parental behaviors considered in this report are listed in Table 5.1 along with their definitions. They were selected on the basis of previous home-based research on mother-infant interaction highlighting developmentally facilitative parental styles (for example, Beckwith 1971; Clarke-Stewart 1973) and research in constrained settings highlighting differences between mother-infant and father-infant interactions (for example, Lamb 1977b; Parke and O'Leary 1976). The procedure for assessing reliability was based upon the rate of interobserver agreement in coding the presence of a behavior in the same 15-second period. Five tests of agreement were carried out in the homes of five (nonstudy) families prior to formal data collection, following four weeks of practice coding

---

*In this regard, Pedersen et al. (1979) have recently commented that "it may be difficult to identify a single slice of time in which to conduct observations of mothers and fathers that represents a psychologically equivalent experience for both parents."

TABLE 5.1

Parent Behavior Variables: Definitions and Reliabilities

Variable Name	Description	Reliablility
Verbal behavior		
Vocalize	Number of 15-second periods in which parent vocalizes to child.	.85
Verbal response rate	Proportion of child's vocalizations to parent that parent verbally responds to.	.88
Nonverbal behavior		
Stimulate	Number of 15-second periods in which parent attempts to focus child's attention on some object or event within the environment (for example, point to something out the window, show picture, give toy).	.86
Restrict	Number of 15-second periods in which parent physically or verbally restricts child's behavior.	.77
Read/watch TV	Number of 15-second periods in which parent reads to self or watches television.	.92
Physical contact		
Caretake	Number of 15- second periods in which parent touches the child in service of providing physical care (for example, change diaper).	.93
Positive affection	Number of 15-second periods in which parent hugs, kisses, or affectionately touches child.	.90

TABLE 5.1 (Continued)

Variable Name	Description	Reliablility
Soothe	Number of 15-second periods in which parent physically contacts child in order to comfort.	1.00
Play	Number of 15-second periods in which parent physically contacts child while playing with him/her.	.89
Simple	Number of 15-second periods in which parent touches child for some other reason, usually to pick up or hold.	.83
Play	All play categories assume interaction between parent and child aimed at mutual enjoyment of each participant.	
Social play	Number of 15-second periods in which social games such as peek-a-boo, and chase are engaged in.	.85
Object-mediated play	Number of 15-second periods in which parent and child engage in playful interaction focused around toy or object.	.89
Vigorous motion play	Number of 15-second periods in which play involves vigorous physical manipulation of the child (for example, tossing child in air, bouncing on knee).	.93

Source: Compiled by the author.

live and videotaped triadic interaction. Across all tests of reliability, percentage agreement (agreements divided by agreements plus disagreements) ranged from 70 to 100 percent (see Table 5.1). The author conducted all observations once adequate levels of interobserver agreement were achieved between himself and an undergraduate assistant.

As behavior scores were summed in terms of the social situation that characterized a 15-second period (mother alone with child, father alone with child, and both parents together),* and as these situations occurred with differential frequency across the families studied due to natural variations in family functioning, all behavior scores were prorated to a standard 30-minute observation period in each situation. These prorated scores were then added together to provide total mother and father scores. Since no differences occurred between observations one and two on any of the parental behaviors, scores for each day were added together.

Exploratory Competence Assessment

Within a week of the second observation, and prior to the infant's 15-month birthday, mother and baby were visited by the now-familiar observer at a time that was scheduled to coincide with a period when the baby was awake, active, and not hungry. Following a 10- to 15-minute reacquaintance period in which the observer conversed with the mother and, if necessary, made arrangements for other household members to leave mother, baby, and experimenter alone, the child was provided with a set of "warm-up" toys (doll, miniature tea set, blocks, cubes) to play with. The purpose of these toys was to familiarize the child with the experience of receiving toys from the experimenter. The play setting was usually the living room or kitchen or some other household area that afforded the experimenter and mother the opportunity to sit comfortably and converse in a neighborly fashion while the child played comfortably at their feet. The intent was to create a situation ecologically analogous to one that might occur in the family's everyday experience and, thereby, enable the child to play at ease.

Following approximately five minutes of play with the warm-up toys, the mother attracted the child's attention with a small bell that she had been given for this purpose. With the child on the mother's lap, the warm-up toys were cleared away by the experimenter who set in their places, in a standard fashion,

---

*Being with the child was defined as being in the same room or in the room adjacent to that containing the child. Data on social situation differences are contained in another report (Belsky 1977).

three "test" toys: a homemade large peg board with two loose plastic rings, a Fischer-Price Chatter Telephone, and a Fischer-Price Queen Buzy Bee. Then the experimenter signaled the mother to allow the child access to the toys. For five minutes, during which the mother was instructed to respond to but not initiate interaction with the child, the baby explored the toys. After five minutes, the experimenter called the child's name to capture his/her attention and set down a fourth "novel" toy: a carnival-colored, flatbed cart on wheels, with four replaceable spoollike rollers, mounted on shafts, that spun when the cart rolled (manufactured in Sweden by Brio). For four additional minutes the child was free to play with any of the available toys. In the event that a child wandered away during any part of the testing session (which few did), mothers were instructed to call the child, tap a toy, and request that she/he return and play some more. Of 40 children observed in this manner, only one whose interest wandered could not be attracted back to the play materials. This child's scores were prorated to reflect a full nine-minute period.*

Throughout the test session, infant exploratory behavior was coded on a continuous ten-second interval basis by means of an 11-category checklist. Ten of the categories, coded "appropriate behaviors" (McCall 1974), were uniquely suited to a particular toy or toys and would not likely occur with other objects: (1) pulling or rolling the bee, telephone, or cart; (2) spinning the wheels of these toys; (3) placing a ring on a wooden peg; (4) inserting a peg in a peg board hole; (5) turning the wings of the Buzy Bee; (6) flipping the antenna of the bee; (7) dialing the phone; (8) "hanging up" the phone receiver; (9) bringing the phone receiver to the ear as if to listen; and (10) placing a spool on one of the shafts of the colorful cart. The eleventh category, labeled "aimless," was coded if the child spent an entire ten-second period uninvolved with either the toys, the experimenter or parent, or any other potentially explorative object in the room (for example, curtains, coffee table). In addition to coding these 11 categories on a ten-second basis, the onset and termination of the child's involvement with each toy was marked on the scoring sheet.

Reliability in coding all play behaviors was established prior to formal data collection. Interobserver agreement (on five live testings, following several weeks of coding videotaped play sessions) was calculated per ten-second period; agreement across the 11 categories and onset and offset times ranged from .82 to .97.

On the basis of the data gathered, four measures of infant exploratory competence were created:

---

*In the case of one child who could not be interested in the warm-up toys at all, it was necessary to return on a second occasion to assess her exploratory competence.

1. Longest duration of sustained activity—the duration (in seconds) of the child's longest bout with any single toy ($\bar{X}$ = 158.6).

2. Aimlessness—the number of ten-second periods in which the child was completely uninvolved in exploratory activity ($\bar{X}$ = 2.4).

3. Appropriate activities—the number of different appropriate behaviors (of the ten listed above) performed by the child ($\bar{X}$ = 5.0).

4. Creativity index—developed from McCall (1974) in the following manner: the ten appropriate behaviors were ranked in reverse order of the number of children performing each behavior. They were then divided into five groups (two behaviors per group) and ranked from least (score 5) to most frequent (score 1). A weighted score was then computed (McCall 1974): "A single child's creativity index was the sum of the number of each type of appropriate behaviors weighted (i.e., multiplied) by its respective infrequency rank in the sample. Thus, the creativity index reflects the extent and uniqueness with which a child played appropriately with the objects." The sample mean was 51.1. In addition to the validation of this weighting system found in McCall's research, the index correlated highly (.94) with ratings of the complexity and difficulty of the behaviors for 15-month-old infants made by five graduate students in developmental psychology.

To determine if observed competence was related to the child's previous experience with the toys employed in the assessment situation, a correlational analysis was performed. No relationships were found between prior experience (number of toys the child owned) and any of the four competence measures. Thus, the data gathered were not biased as a function of the availability of any of the materials used.

RESULTS AND DISCUSSION

Similarities Between Mother and Father

The data concerning mean frequencies of observed maternal and paternal behavior will be examined first. As Table 5.2 reveals, when the behavior scores for each parent were summed across dyadic and triadic situations and compared, few mean differences emerged. Indeed, of the 13 parental variables subjected to analysis, only two significantly differentiated between parents, with mothers more frequently stimulating—$F(1, 33)$ = 4.80, $p < .05$—and taking physical care of their infants, $F(1, 33)$ = 9.87, $p < .01$. It should be noted, however, that both of these main effects were qualified by higher-order interactions. In the case of the measure stimulate, a parent by sex of child interaction indicated that mothers and fathers alike preferred to interact with their same-sexed children, $F(1, 33)$ = 6.41, $p < .05$; a similar effect emerged with respect to the expression of positive

TABLE 5.2

Mean Frequencies of Parental Behaviors

	Mother	Father	Significance Level of Difference
Verbal behavior			
Vocalize to	105	106	n. s.
Verbal response rate	37	39	n. s.
Nonverbal behavior			
Stimulate[a]	34	54	.05
Restrict	9	7	n. s.
Read/watch TV	16	33	n. s.
Play			
Social	8	11	n. s.
Object-mediated	4	7	n. s.
Vigorous motion	2	4	n. s.
Physical contact			
Simple	26	36	n. s.
Caretake[b]	11	4	.01
Positive affection[b]	4	3	n. s.
Soothe	2	1	n. s.
Play	8	15	n. s.

[a]Significant parent by sex of child interaction; see text.
[b]Significant parent by social situation interaction; see text.
Source: Compiled by the author.

affect, $F(1, 33) = 7.61, p < .01$. With regard to caretaking, a significant parent by situation interaction highlighted the fact that, although mothers exceeded fathers in caretaking in both dyadic and triadic situations, the differences between parents were most marked in the former context, $F(1, 33) = 5.91, p < .05$; a similar interaction emerged with respect to positive affection, $F(1, 33) = 4.13$, $p < .05$. In summary, the results of these mother-father comparisons clearly indicate that similarities far outweigh differences in the manner in which mothers and fathers from traditional nuclear families interact with their 15-month-old infants.

TABLE 5.3

Significant Pearson Product Moment Correlations Between Exploratory Competence Measures and Maternal/Paternal Behaviors

	Competence Measures			
	Longest Sustained Activity	Period of Aimlessness	Appropriate Behaviors	Creativity Index
Maternal behaviors				
Total vocalizations				
Verbal response rate				
Stimulate			.36	
Restrict				
Read/watch TV				
Simple touch	−.44			
Soothe				
Caretake				
Positive affection				
Play touch				.41
Object play	.31			
Social play	.35			.44
Vigorous motion play				
Paternal behaviors				
Total vocalizations	.51	−.32		.62
Verbal response rate		−.39		
Stimulate				.32
Restrict				
Read/watch TV		.41		
Simple touch				
Soothe				.32
Caretake	.39			
Positive affection	.42			.56
Play touch			.40	.37
Object play				
Social play				
Vigorous motion play				.38

Note: N = 40, $r \geqslant .31$: $p < .05$; $r \geqslant .40$: $p < .01$.
Source: Compiled by the author.

Relations Between Parental Behavior
and Exploratory Competence

In order to compare the interrelation of mothering and fathering with infant exploratory competence, the 13 parental behaviors listed in Table 5.1 were intercorrelated with the four measures of infant competence. The results of this analysis, which are displayed in Table 5.3, reveal more associations that are significant between patterns of fathering and infant development than between patterns of mothering and infant competence. Specifically, while only 12 percent of the mother-infant correlations achieved statistical significance ($p < .05$), 25 percent of the father-infant coefficients reached this criterion ($r > .31$). Paternal behaviors associated with infant competence show their most striking concentration of relationships with the creativity index.

There was one instance where there was an exact replication for mothers and fathers in the significant relationship between parental behavior and measure of infant competence, the correlations between physical contact in play and the creativity index. The parental behavior, stimulate, in which an attempt is made to focus the child's attention on some object or event in the environment, shows a suggestive replication in being associated with the category of competence, appropriate behaviors, when provided by mothers and the creativity index when provided by fathers.

These results support previous findings on cognitive socialization in infancy (for example, Beckwith 1971; Clarke-Stewart 1973; Yarrow, Rubenstein, and Pedersen 1975) and not only extend the work on parental influence into the realm of fathering but also highlight some of the processes through which both mother and father may affect their infant's development. The correlations between parental stimulation and infant competence, for example, are considered to be a function of the attention-focusing properties of this parental behavior and the attentional demands of the play assessment. Specifically, the toddler's capacity to extract from the objects information inherent within them (that is, by displaying appropriate behaviors) is hypothesized to result from his or her previous experience in having attention directed and focused by parents. What is being proposed is that in stimulating their infants, mothers and fathers teach their young children how to stimulate themselves and focus their own attention.

The relationship between physical contact during play and exploratory competence is thought to be the result of a motivational rather than an attentional process. In accordance with certain of Erikson's (1950) formulations concerning the development of basic trust, the pleasure and arousal that commonly accompanies physical contact is assumed to extend beyond the immediate interaction between parent and infant. In so doing, it serves to enhance the child's curiosity and motivation to explore the world. This interpretation represents a restatement of Erikson's developmental model of early ego development in which industry and initiative are seen to be ontogenetically rooted in pleasurable social interaction.

Additional support for this interpretation of data presented in Table 5.3 can be found in the recent work of Yarrow and his colleagues concerning the development and assessment of mastery motivation in infancy. In examining the contemporaneous relationships between maternal behavior at six months and cognitive-motivational performance on the Bayley Mental Development Scale, these researchers reported positive and significant associations between frequency of kinesthetic stimulation and instances of secondary circular reactions and goal-directed behavior (Yarrow, Rubenstein, and Pedersen 1975). Follow-up assessments of children studied in this investigation revealed, moreover, that mastery displayed in several experimental play situations at 12 months (see Yarrow et al. 1978, for descriptions) was more systematically related to this category of maternal behavior than any other coded at 6 months (Yarrow 1976). When these data are juxtaposed to those presented above, they clearly suggest that pleasurable physical contact between infants and their parents fosters curiosity and facilitates the development of exploratory skill.

One other similarity between the mother-infant and father-infant correlations is the absence of a significant association between maternal or paternal restrictions and exploratory competence. This failure to replicate previous work indicating that infants with restrictive mothers perform less well on standardized assessments of infant development (for example, Beckwith 1971; Clarke-Stewart 1973; Carew et al. 1975; Wachs 1976) may be a function of the relatively low levels of restriction that were observed. Despite this possibility, we shall see in a subsequent analysis that, when parents are considered as a unit rather than as individual agents of influence, high levels of restrictions are indeed associated with poorer performance in the play situation.

Selective Parent-Infant Associations

Having commented on the similarities between the mother-infant and father-infant correlations, the more evident differences that emerged from this analysis will now be considered. In all, four trends were discerned: one concerns play; two involve physical contact; and the last, verbal behavior.

In the realm of play, differences in maternal and paternal correlations with infant competence tended to mirror mean parental differences that have been observed in other investigations of parenting during infancy (Clarke-Stewart, Chapter 6, this volume; Lamb, Chapter 2, this volume). That is, those areas of play in which mothers have been observed to excel (namely, object-mediated and social play) were found to be related to infant competence—but only for mothers. Similarly, that area of play in which fathers have been observed to excel (that is, vigorous motion play) was found to be related to infant competence, but, once again, only for fathers (see Table 5.3). While other investigators have stressed that parents differ in the frequency with which they engage in certain types of play with their infants, the present results show that differential play styles have differential consequences as well.

It appears that maternal object-mediated play directly promotes the child's attention to inanimate objects, such as the stimulus materials employed in the present study, reflected in long durations of sustained activity. The relationships between maternal social play (for example, peek-a-boo, tickling) and duration of sustained activity as well as creativity, on the other hand, are probably a function of the arousing and hedonic (and thus motivating) properties that such social interaction frequently embodies. If Watson (1972) is correct in his analysis of social games, moreover, the response-contingent nature of such play may also facilitate the development of exploratory competence by engendering within the young child the sense of environmental control (compare Lewis and Goldberg 1969). Finally, the relationship between paternal vigorous motion play and the uniqueness of the child's appropriate behaviors (that is, creativity score) stems, in all likelihood, from the extremely arousing and pleasurable effects of such experiences as being tossed in the air, swung by the arms, and bounced on one's knees. Arousing social interaction is hypothesized to exert a motivating influence that extends beyond the immediate interactive situation.

Differences in maternal and paternal associations with infant competence are also evident in the various domains of physical contact. Several competence measures were positively related to the frequency with which fathers—but not mothers—hugged and kissed (positive affection), took physical care of (caretake), and comforted their children (soothe). To the extent that these behaviors can be considered traditionally maternal, infants with fathers likely to display these behaviors may benefit because they are receiving something special or extra. Further, many of these behaviors involve warm, loving contact between father and child and, thus, can be considered to promote basic trust and, thereby, industry and initiative (Erikson 1950).

Mother and father also differed in their effects associated with another measure of physical contact—that labeled "simple touch." Though fathers' basic holding was unrelated to competent performance in the play situation, the more mothers were observed to hold their infants in this fashion during the naturalistic observations, the shorter were their toddlers' lengthiest concentration spans during the play assessment ($r = -.44$). If such holding is primarily a function of maternal rather than child need at this age, this negative relationship between parental behavior and infant competence may result from the fact that infants, while being held, are simultaneously being denied the learning experiences that come through more active social interaction or exploration of the inanimate environment.

The final trend discerned from the correlations displayed in Table 5.3 may be the most informative, as it suggests that general paternal involvement is associated with competent exploration. More specifically, several individual correlations indicate that fathers who are actively involved with their toddlers (a evidenced by frequent talking and high rates of verbal responsiveness) have children who exhibit little aimlessness and high levels of creativity, whereas those whose fathers spend large amounts of time involved in solitary pursuits (watching television, reading to themselves) have children who have difficulty getting and/or staying involved in exploration.

To summarize these findings, the separate analysis of maternal and paternal influences highlights similarities as well as differences in the manner in which mothers and fathers may promote exploratory competence. Fathers who frequently talked to, verbally responded to, stimulated, kissed and hugged, and took physical care of their infants, as well as frequently engaged them in vigorous motion play and infrequently participated in solitary activities, had infants who performed competently in the play situation. Those infants whose mothers frequently stimulated and engaged them in object-mediated and social play but infrequently held them for no apparent reason (simple touch) also performed competently.

Comparisons of Patterns of Maternal and Paternal Behavior in Relation to Exploratory Competence

The analyses presented in Table 5.3 treated mothers and fathers as separate classes of parents, tracing relations between parental behavior and the infant's exploratory competence. These data were not analyzed in a fashion that preserved the information that each mother-infant and father-infant pair existed in a distinct combination, mother and father to the same child. Pedersen and his colleagues have argued, however, (Pedersen et al. 1979) that it might be profitable to make statistical evaluations of parental effects utilizing the family as the unit of analysis, since it is with a unique combination of parents that the infant's experiences occur. The effects of the father's behavior should be evaluated, not just in comparison with mothers in general, but in combination with the particular mother with whom he shares care for the child.

There are a variety of statistical strategies for evaluating the combined impact of mother and father. One which seems logical is multiple regression analysis in which two parent scores could be employed jointly as predictors of competence. A decision was made to forgo this procedure on the grounds that it presumes linear summational effect. This investigator's own intuition suggested that the patterning of maternal and paternal behavior within a family might more accurately characterize their combined influence than a scheme (like multiple regression) that simply adds to one parent's influence the nonredundant contribution of the second parent. Moreover, the weighting of each parent's contribution in multiple regression is determined by the intercorrelations of measures, an index reflecting sample characteristics, not the unique combinations of behaviors that a mother and father have by virtue of being in the same family. Specifically, what was considered most potentially influential was the experience that the juxtaposition of mothering and fathering styles created for the child. Given this hunch, the decision was made to employ the analytic strategy recently proposed by Pedersen et al. (1979) that presumes such a combinatorial model of family influence. This procedure involves classifying families according to the naturally occurring combinations of parental behavior on any dimension or set of dimensions. By dividing the distributions of scores of parental characteristics at the median, family "types" are created in which, for example, both mother and father are above the median or both parents are below the median; there are two other combinations with one parent above and the other below the median. Outcome characteristics, such as measures of the child's behavior, are then evaluated for the various combinations of parenting styles.

Family Analysis I

On the basis of the correlational patterns already examined for mothers and fathers, several predictions were made with respect to what kinds of family parenting patterns would be associated with the highest and lowest levels of infant exploratory competence. Four specific predictions were made: (1) that infants whose mothers frequently engaged them in social play and whose fathers frequently participated in vigorous motion play would perform best on the competence assessment, whereas those whose respective parents each scored low on these playful activities would perform least competently; (2) that infants whose mothers frequently engaged in object-mediated play and whose fathers frequently displayed positive affection toward them would perform most competently, whereas those whose respective parents scored low on these parental measures would perform least competently; (3) that infants whose mothers were infrequently observed to simply hold them and whose fathers frequently participated in vigorous motion play would perform most competently, whereas those whose respective parents behaved in the reverse fashion would perform least competently; and, finally, (4) that those infants whose mothers infrequently held them and whose fathers frequently engaged them in vigorous motion play would perform most competently, whereas those whose respective parents behaved in reverse fashion would perform least competently.

On each of the maternal and paternal measures included in these predictions, the sample of mothers and fathers, respectively, were divided in half at the median. For example, a father who scored above the father median on the variable, positive affection, fell into the Father High (Hi) group. Similarly, a mother whose frequency of simply holding the baby fell below the maternal median on this behavior was categorized in the Mother Low (Lo) group. Thus, in each family each parent's score on the behavior of concern was categorized as high or low relative to the performance of the other mothers or fathers.

TABLE 5.4

Mean Infant Competence Scores as a Function of Selected Mother-Father Median Split Comparisons

Paired Mother-Father Behaviors	Longest Sustained Activity					Creativity Index				
	M. Hi F. Hi	M. Hi F. Lo	M. Lo F. Hi	M. Lo F. Lo	t^a	M. Hi F. Hi	M. Hi F. Lo	M. Lo F. Hi	M. Lo F. Lo	t^a
M. Social play[b] F. Vigorous motion play	$209.6^{c,d}$	153.8	152.2	$121.8^{d,e}$	3.49^f	$72.1^{c,d}$	46.5	44.9	$41.2^{d,e}$	1.99^g
M. Object play[h] F. Positive affection	$192.7^{c,d}$	178.9	131.8	$129.6^{d,e}$	2.37^g	$56.8^{c,d}$	51.2	55.0	$41.0^{d,e}$	1.25
M. Simple touch[i] F. Read/watch TV	140.8^d	145.0	150.4	$190.9^{c,d}$	2.69^f	$43.7^{d,e}$	39.4	42.2	$72.3^{c,d}$	2.03^g
M. Simple touch[j] F. Vigorous motion play	145.5	$138.9^{d,e}$	$183.8^{c,d}$	165.6	1.37^k	48.5	$34.0^{d,e}$	$64.0^{c,d}$	56.5	1.82^g

[a]Comparison of predicted highest versus predicted lowest means–one-tailed t test.
[b]Respective family group numbers: 10, 10, 9, 11.
[c]Predicted highest mean.
[d]Scores confirmed predictions.
[e]Predicted lowest mean.
[f]$p < .01$.
[g]$p < .05$.
[h]Respective family group numbers: 11, 9, 10, 10.
[i]Respective family group numbers: 12, 8, 8, 12.
[j]Respective family group numbers: 11, 9, 10, 10.
[k]$p < .10$.
Note: M. = mother; F. = father; Hi = high; Lo = low.
Source: Compiled by the author.

To evaluate the predictions, mean competence scores were calculated for infants from families of each type as determined by the combinations of maternal and paternal behaviors. To test each hypothesis, the average performance of infants whose behavior was predicted to be most competent—as a function of the type of family from which they came—was compared (via one-tailed t tests) to that of infants reared in the type of family predicted to be least supportive of exploratory competence. Because this procedure was considered exploratory, only the two measures of competence that evidenced the most consistent association with parental behavior in the separate maternal and paternal correlational analyses were employed in these comparisons: longest duration of sustained activity and creativity.

The results of these comparisons, which clearly highlight the potential power of a family analysis, are displayed in Table 5.4. Not only were seven of eight predictions of best performance and worst performance confirmed, an accuracy rate that is highly significant ($X^2 = 121.0, p < .0001$), but six of eight of these predicted best performance–worst performance scores were significantly different ($p < .05$).

Family Analysis II

Having achieved such positive results by selecting combinations of variables that the correlational analyses suggested would be particularly potent, it was decided to explore separately the effects of each of the 13 parental behaviors. Four family types were created, as before, by juxtaposing the various combinations of maternal and paternal behavior rates. This time, however, a more stringent criterion of exploratory competence was employed; mean infant competence scores were calculated for each family type defined on each of the 13 measures for all four exploratory competence measures. A family type was identified as most promoting of infant exploratory competence if the infants from those families averaged the lengthiest duration of sustained activity, the fewest periods of aimlessness, the largest number of appropriate behaviors, *and* the highest creativity scores. In other words, for a family type to be identified as most or least promoting of infant exploratory competence, children from these families had to average the most or least competent performance on every one of the four measures.

Given this rather strict criterion for characterizing a family as most or least promoting of competence, it was possible to identify such families on 10 of 13 parental variables. Specifically, children from families in which both parents scored above the median (Hi-Hi) on the variables of positive affection, play touch, and vigorous motion play were found to have the lengthiest episodes of sustained activity, exhibit the highest number of appropriate behaviors, show the greatest creativity, and have the fewest periods of aimlessness. In families in which both parents scored above the median on the variable read/watch TV, in contrast, infants consistently exhibited the least competent exploration. Considered together, these patterns indicate that children from families in which both mother and father are actively involved in parenting develop into the most competent explorers. Additional evidence in support of this interpretation is found in data demonstrating that those families in which both parents scored below their respective medians (Lo-Lo group) on the variables of total vocalizations, verbal response rate, social play, and vigorous motion play had infants who consistently performed least competently on all four measures of exploratory skill.

The least competent explorers were also found to be from families in which both mother and father were highly restrictive (Hi-Hi), indicating that considerations of quantity of parental involvement must be balanced by a concern for the quality of parenting. When parental activity is characterized by frequent prohibitions, it appears that infants' exploratory skills suffer, possibly because their curiosity and thus motivation to explore is inhibited. This relationship between exploratory competence and restriction is considered especially important not only for the light it sheds upon the possible processes by which exploratory competence develops but also because it highlights once again the power of a family analysis of parenting; the separate correlational analyses of maternal and paternal behavior evidenced no relationship between restriction and competence (see Table 5.3).

In contrast to these rather straightforward results, in which the Hi-Hi families appear so readily distinguishable from the Lo-Lo families, there was one other unique constellation of parental behavior rates that emerged for the variables of total vocalizations, verbal response rate, stimulation, and simple touch. Children who scored consistently highest on all four competence measures came from families in which mother scored below the median and father scored above the median on these behaviors (Lo-Hi group).

To test the reliability of these unexpected patterns, each infant's score on the four individual competence measures was standardized and combined in order to create a total competence score (longest sustained activity plus appropriate behaviors plus creativity index minus periods of aimlessness). A mean total competence score was then calculated for each of the four family types on the four parental variables for which the Lo-Hi pattern emerged. The mean scores of the Lo-Hi group were then tested, via a posteriori t comparisons, against the other three groups. The results of this analysis are displayed in Table 5.5. Infants from the Mother Lo–Father Hi group scored significantly higher than those from the other family types on the total competence score, thus confirming the reliability of these unexpected patterns.

The intriguing question remains why certain categories of parental behavior, occurring in the Hi-Hi pattern, are most promoting of exploratory competence, while other variables must occur in the Mother Lo–Father Hi pattern for similar effects to be observed. One possible interpretation relates to the relative

TABLE 5.5

Mean Total Competence Scores as a Function of Family Groups on Selected Parent Variables

	Family Groups				
Parent Variables	M. Hi F. Hi	M. Hi F. Lo	M. Lo F. Hi	M. Lo F. Lo	t^a (df = 36)
Total vocalization	.77	.06	1.71	-2.19	2.17^b
Verbal response rate	.49	.15	2.05	-2.00	2.49^c
Stimulation	-.41	-.30	2.14	-.77	2.45^c
Simple touch	-.39	-1.06	1.12	.33	1.46^d

[a]Predicted highest (M. Lo-F. Hi) versus all other scores combined—one-tailed t test.
[b]$p < .05$.
[c]$p < .01$.
[d]$p < .10$.

Note: Total competence = longest sustained activity plus appropriate behaviors plus creativity index minus periods of aimlessness; M = mother, F = father; Hi = high; Lo = low.

Source: Compiled by the author.

frequencies with which these behaviors occurred. It appears that the variables for which the Lo-Hi pattern was associated with highest exploratory competence—total vocalizations, verbal response rate, stimulation, and simple touch—are ones that are high in absolute frequency of occurrence (see Table 5.2). Variables for which the Hi-Hi pattern was associated with highest exploratory competence, in contrast, have a relatively low frequency of occurrence—positive affection, play touch, and vigorous motion play. The former set of variables also was conceptualized as general indexes of parental involvement, whereas the latter set was pinpointed as especially arousing and pleasurable to the infant.

On the basis of these differentiations, it appears that infants from the Mother Lo-Father Hi group excel because they are afforded the optimal balance between parental attention and freedom to exercise their developing autonomy. That is, while their mothers' relatively low levels of involvement (which should be considered moderate rather than minimal in the middle-class families studied), exercised across the entire day, provide them with a great deal of opportunity to explore while at the same time meeting their emotional needs; their fathers' high levels of involvement, exercised only a limited part of the day, serve to fuel their motivation to explore. The key to understanding the difference between maternal and paternal involvement seems to be the parents' differential availability to the child. Too high a level of mothering, administered over a long period, seems to stifle the child, whereas a great deal of fathering, administered over a fairly brief period of time, has just the opposite influence. Thus, low levels of maternal involvement, coupled with high levels of paternal involvement, result in family styles most supportive of exploratory competence.

As noted earlier, this same family pattern does not account for the most competent performance when parenting behaviors are relatively low in absolute frequency but tend to be highly arousing—most probably because they occur with such sufficient infrequency that they cannot overwhelm the young child. Put another way, the occurrence of such stimulating and affectively laden parenting styles is sufficiently rare, even at its maximum, so that the infant does not appear to benefit from some limitation on this kind of parental activity. Quite the contrary, it appears that more of such behavior—from both mother and father—is associated with higher competence levels.

In summary, infant exploratory competence appears to develop best in families in which mothers are moderately involved in parenting and fathers are highly involved and in which both parents frequently engage their toddlers in highly arousing and positively affective social interaction.

CONCLUSIONS

In addition to providing documentation of the ways in which fathers may influence their infants' motivation to explore and contribute to their skill in exploring, the results of the present investigation add to our understanding of infant development by demonstrating the potential power of a family analysis of early experience. For in examining the differential and combined impact of mother and father on infant exploratory competence, the present study clearly demonstrates that consideration of mother and father as a family unit adds much to our understanding of parental influence. That this is the case should not be surprising; after all, the mother-infant relationship does not exist within a vacuum. Rather, it is imbedded within a family system that encompasses a father-infant relationship as well. And, as the results of the present investigation suggest, the influence of mother on the infant should be considered within the context of father's influence.

In evaluating the strategy of creating various patterns of parental behavior to assess the combined influence of mother and father on infant exploratory competence, it is clear that the approach suggested by Pedersen et al. (1979) is only one of several possibilities. Multiple regression analysis is an alternative strategy. Moreover, patterns can be created by comparing the relative standing of mother to father within a family, rather than in terms of the separate distributions of scores for mothers and fathers. That is, families could have been categorized as mother equals father, mother greater than father, or mother less than father on any single behavior or combination of several, depending upon how maternal behavior compares with paternal behavior within a family. At present, the empirical implications of the various alternatives are not fully understood, and there is great need for theoretical development to guide future research. One hope of the present study is that it will serve to stimulate such theorizing.

Serious consideration of the family as a system implies more than that the father-infant relationship be considered while examining the nature and consequences of the mother-infant relationship. As the ground-breaking work of Pedersen and his colleagues has demonstrated (Pedersen, Anderson, and Cain, Chapter 4, this volume) as has the work of Price (1977) and Belsky (in press), the inclusion of father in the study of infancy not only transforms the mother-infant dyad into the mother-father-infant triad, but, in so doing, it draws attention to spousal relations in addition to parent-infant relations. In order to achieve complete understanding of the nature and consequence of family experience during infancy, then, serious attention must be devoted to both the spousal and parental units. The "unexpressed working arrangement" that Aldous (1977) has noted between family sociologists and developmental psychologists, whereby the former concern themselves with the husband-wife relationship and the latter the parent-child relationship, must be renegotiated. By working from an interdisciplinary perspective, human ecologists can enhance their insights into the infant's experience in the family and, thereby, advance their understanding of influences upon development.

Such advances would have practical as well as scientific implications. In addition to increased understanding of infant development, new approaches to early intervention might eventuate. The strategies that have been employed to date to enhance development of high-risk infants through environmental manipulation have generally focused upon only the infant or the mother-infant relationship (for example, Bronfenbrenner 1974b; Kessen and Fein 1975; Lambie, Bond, and Weikart 1974; Levenstein 1970). Though several parallels between research on the mother-infant and father-infant relationships are apparent, in the area of intervention almost no parallels exist. As far as the author is aware, only Zelazo et al. (1977) have attempted to intervene with fathers to influence infant development. Though their limited four-week effort to promote infant attachment to father proved unsuccessful (as indexed by pre- and post-intervention assessments of attachment in the "strange situation"), the originality of their attempt makes it noteworthy.

Given the general absence of informal socialization for fatherhood relative to motherhood and the low baseline levels of much father involvement, it is possible that the parenting of fathers may be more susceptible to influence than that of mothers. In light of the findings emerging from this report, moreover, it is also reasonable to hypothesize that interventions that succeed in increasing the quality as well as quantity of fathering could enhance infant development.

The emphasis here on interventions with fathers should not make us lose sight of the overriding theme of this book—namely, the importance of considering mother and father together as a family system. In fact, it may be that interventions geared toward both parents will prove more successful than any directed to mother or father alone. Further, there is no reason why intervention in infancy could not focus upon the spousal dyad as well as each individual parent.

Finally, there are implications of considering mother and father as a family unit in regard to the observational methodologies employed in this and other studies of parent-infant interaction. To date, investigators have concentrated their efforts on capturing, at a molecular behavioral level, the interactions of mothers, fathers, and infants. Rarely have attempts been made to characterize the nature of the family system at more abstract levels of description, though appeals to do so have been made (compare Bronfenbrenner 1977). Levels of description that have proved useful for the investigation of parent-infant interaction may not necessarily be the most useful for studying the larger family system. Moreover, methodologies for studying parental influence on infant development implicitly assume that the young child derives experience in molecular units associated with individual persons, but there seems no overwhelming theoretical or empirical reason to believe this is the case. Such questioning of traditional strategies for studying the parent-infant relationship, coupled with a serious appreciation of a family analysis, should pave the way for advances in our understanding of infancy.

6

THE FATHER'S CONTRIBUTION TO CHILDREN'S COGNITIVE AND SOCIAL DEVELOPMENT IN EARLY CHILDHOOD

K. Alison Clarke-Stewart

In the late 1970s, as mothers, more and more, have taken over classrooms and conferences, boardrooms and businesses, fathers have made their appearance in kitchens and kindergartens, labor rooms and nurseries, and now, finally, are making their mark in the annals of child development research. As recently as 1975, fathers were labeled "forgotten contributors to child development" by the child development community (Lamb 1975a), but now that appellation no longer holds. The present volume reflects a small but growing literature focused on fathers—their roles, their thoughts, their behavior, their contributions to children's development. Psychological researchers increasingly are concerned with the family unit beyond the mother-child dyad, and research on fathers, previously limited to evaluation of the effects of paternal absence, now includes a number of direct investigations of fathers' attitudes and behavior.

The earliest of these investigations attempts to demonstrate empirically how active and involved fathers are with their infants. Perhaps in reaction to society's devaluation of the paternal role, the agenda of these studies seems to be to assert that fathers are more nurturant than stereotypes of men suggest. Research findings indicate that fathers are "engrossed" in their infants (Greenberg and Morris 1974) and as nurturant, affectionate, and active with them as mothers (Parke and O'Leary 1976). But the contrived nature of some observations may have limited generalizations; although studies show that fathers can be as active as mothers when interaction is clearly expected and

This research was supported by a grant from the Office of Child Development (OCD-CB-98) to William Kessen and Greta Fein, Yale University. Some parts of the chapter first appeared in an article entitled "And Daddy Makes Three: The Father's Impact on Mother and Young Child," *Child Development*, 1978, *49*, 466-478.

an observer is taking notes, they do not establish how much fathers actually care for their infants in the natural home environment. Independent parental reports (Ban and Lewis 1964; Kotelchuck 1976; Lewis and Weinraub 1974; Pedersen and Robson 1969) suggest that fathers' nurturant behavior in the home is more circumscribed.

In addition to demonstrating how much fathers were like mothers, investigations also showed differences. Differences between men's and women's responses to children have been documented (Berman 1976). To explain such findings, differences in the biological "connectedness" of mothers and fathers were noted (Lewis and Weinraub 1976). It was suggested that, because of the biological link between mother and infant, the mother's effect was more likely to be "direct" and her role to involve physical caregiving, while the father's effect was more likely to be "indirect" and his role to involve playful interactions and a link to the outside world (Lamb 1976g; Lewis and Weinraub 1976). Supporting these hypotheses, Kotelchuck (1976) offered documentation from parental interviews that father-child interaction was more likely than mother-child interaction to involve play and mother-child interaction to involve caretaking; Lamb (Chapter 2, this volume) presented evidence that these differential interaction patterns existed in natural interaction at home. In his observations, fathers were more likely to hold their infants for play while mothers held them for caretaking. Further information about differential parental play styles was offered by Lytton (1976), Weinraub and Frankel (1977), and Yogman (1977). Fathers' play, in these studies, was more physical, idiosyncratic, and unpredictable, and mothers' play, more conventional and related to materials; fathers' play involved physical tapping (with infants) or romping (with toddlers), while mothers' play was more verbal.

As well as investigating differences in parental styles, researchers probed differences in children's reactions to mother and father. Differences in physical proximity and contact, vocalization and visual attention, and the child's responsiveness to play with the parent were observed and used as indirect evidence for differences in parental styles of interaction (Cohen and Campos 1974; Feldman and Ingham 1975; Lytton 1976; Lamb, Chapter 2, this volume).

Differences in children's behavior to mother and father were also interpreted in the context of children's social development, particularly the development of an "attachment" relation with each parent. In evaluating attachment relationships, a key distinction has been made between attachment and affiliative behavior (Bretherton and Ainsworth 1974). The two behavior systems employ different responses and serve different psychological functions. Attachment behaviors involve physical contact and proximity maintenance for tension-reduction purposes, while affiliative behaviors, such as looking, talking, smiling, and play, are components of friendly social interaction with people who are not exclusively attachment figures. Research findings (Lamb, Chapter 2, this volume) suggest that attachment behaviors, when differential, are more often directed to the mother. In contrast, affiliative behaviors are more often directed to the father. Lamb's observations showed that infants from seven months to two years looked, smiled, and vocalized at father more than at mother in nonstressful, unstructured interactions and responded more positively to play with the father. Further, evidence of differential behavior was provided by Keller's et al. (1975) observation that one-year-olds preferentially looked and vocalized to the fathers in a laboratory/attachment situation. The case was not clear-cut, however. Ban and Lewis (1964) and Feldman and Ingham (1975) reported that in their laboratory situation one-year-olds smiled and vocalized more to mother than to father. It is not clear what factors account for these seemingly discrepant findings, but it is possible that the affiliative preference of children for either parent may have been partly a function of the parent's behavior directed to the child.

The supposition of researchers demonstrating differences in parents' or children's behavior to parents is, of course, that mothers and fathers have different influences on children's development. Unfortunately, research to support this hypothesis, by correlating maternal and paternal variables with assessment of the child's development, has been rare and inconclusive. Too often, investigators of parental predictors of development have either limited their sights to examining maternal behavior in isolation from paternal behavior (see review by Clarke-Stewart 1977) or focused only on the father-child relation, ignoring the concurrent contribution of the mother (for example, Epstein and Radin 1975; Radin 1973). To understand parental influences on children's development, it is necessary to examine children's relations with both mother and father simultaneously, treating the family as a triadic system. This suggests a research approach that gives attention to all the possible relations within the family, looking for similarities as well as differences between parents, for indirect as well as direct effects of parental attitudes and behavior on children's development.

Such an approach was followed in the investigations reported in this volume. In the present study, relations between behaviors of mother and child, father and child, and mother and father were examined as they changed developmentally. In addition, data were collected to assess both similarities and differences in children's attachment and affiliation to mother and father and mothers' and fathers' attitudes and interaction with their children.

METHOD

The data were collected in a longitudinal study of 14 children carried out in 1972–73. Children in the study were randomly selected from hospital birth records and their parents invited by letter to participate in a study of children's normal activities and development from 1 to 2.5 years of age. The first 14 families who agreed to participate constituted the sample. They were all white but included various socioeconomic levels: six families could be categorized as working-class; five, as middle-class; and three, as professional-class. All fathers were employed full time; all mothers were their children's primary caregivers and did not work outside the home. There were seven boys and seven girls in the study, all were first- or second-born. Data were gathered in five different ways: unstructured "natural" observations, semistructured "probe" situations, records kept by mothers, attitude questionnaires completed by both parents, and standardized developmental tests.

Natural Observations

Six one-hour observations were made of the children as they behaved naturally and spontaneously at home; three, when both mother and father were home; and three, when mother was the only parent present. (Although children's behavior when father is the only parent present is of theoretical interest, natural observations of that situation were not included in this investigation because of the relative infrequency of the father-alone condition in the normal lives of these families.) The visits occurred when the children were approximately 15, 20, and 30 months of age, ages selected to both overlap and extend previous research on father-child interaction. They were scheduled in pairs of father-present/father-absent visits within three weeks of each other; the father-present visits were done on weekend days and preceded the father-absent visits in approximately half the pairs.

Before the observation, parents were instructed to ignore the observer and go about their normal activities as far as possible, while the observer followed and recorded the activities of the child. Observation recording was done according to the system of continuous recording in two-columned notebooks described by Clarke-Stewart (1973). Abbreviations for behaviors of the child selected from a preestablished behavior repertoire (for example, looks, clings, holds, gives, plays physically) were written in the right column; those of the persons with whom the child interacted in the left; simultaneous behaviors, on the same line; sequential behaviors, on alternate lines. The observational record was marked in ten-second intervals, at the sound of a beeper in the observer's ear, and any behavior was recorded only once during a ten-second period (unless it was interrupted by another behavior and then resumed). Each behavior was indexed as "R" (responsive) when it occurred in direct response to the behavior of the other person.

The data thus recorded were then manipulated in several ways:

1. To obtain comparable data for all subjects, behavior frequencies were tallied and divided by the total number of ten-second periods in the observation

TABLE 6.1

Variables from Natural Observations

Variable Name	Description	Reliability
Child variables		
Looks	Number of ten-second periods in which C looks at P.	.56
Vocalizes	Number of ten-second periods in which C vocalizes or talks to P.	.75
Looks/in room	Number of ten-second periods in which C looks at P as proportion of time they are in same room.	.68
Vocalizes/in room	Number of ten-second periods in which C vocalizes or talks to P as proportion of time they are in same room.	.69
Smiles/in room	Number of ten-second periods in which C smiles at P as proportion of time they are in same room (C-initiated).	.68
Touches/in room	Number of ten-second periods in which C initiates physical contact with P (touches, holds, clings) as proportion of time they are in same room.	.42
Plays/in room	Number of ten-second periods in which C gives, shows, offers, or plays with toy or object with P as a proportion of time they are in same room (C-initiated).	.56
Plays R/in room	Number of ten-second periods in which C gives, shows, offers, takes, or plays with toy or object with P, plays physically, socially, or a game with P responsively, as a proportion of time they are in same room (P-initiated).	.48
Responsiveness	Proportion of P's social-expressive behaviors (for example, smiles, gives, comes, shows) to which C responded positively (for example, smiles R, takes R, plays R) within same or next ten seconds.	.62
Physical contact	Number of ten-second periods in which P initiates physical contact with C—touches, holds, carries.	.45
Verbal initiation	Number of ten-second periods in which P initiates speech to C.	.73

115

TABLE 6.1 Continued

Variable Name	Description	Reliability
Verbal R	Number of ten-second periods in which P responds to C verbally.	.79
Verbal positive	Number of ten-second periods in which P says something to C that is positive in content and/or tone.	.42
Verbal/in room	Number of ten-second periods in which P initiates speech to C as a proportion of time they are in same room.	.64
Negative behavior	Number of ten-second periods in which P says something to C that is negative in content and/or tone (for example, sharp rebuke or physically punishes C by hitting, slapping, spanking, et cetera).	.76
Plays social	Number of ten-second periods in which P plays physically, socially, or a game with C (P-initiated).	.50
Plays object	Number of ten-second periods in which P gives, shows, offers, plays with toy or object with C (P-initiated).	.74

Plays/in room	Number of ten-second periods in which P gives, shows, offers, plays with toy or object, plays physically, socially, or a game C, as a proportion of time they are in same room (P-initiated).	.49
Social R/in room	Number of ten-second periods in which P touches, holds, caresses, plays socially, physically, or a game with C responsively (C-initiated).	.69
Play proportion	Proportion of ten-second periods that were playful in which P interacted with C (plays social, physical, game, or with object).	.70
Responsiveness	Proportion of C's social-expressive behaviors (for example, smiles, goes to P, gives, shows, kisses) to which P responded positively within the same or next ten seconds (for example, smiles R, plays R, takes R, caresses R, kisses R).	.42
Same room	Number of ten-second periods in which P was visible to and in same room as C.	.67
Interaction duration	Mean length, in ten-second periods, of P-C interaction "episodes" (separated by two or more ten-second periods during which no interaction occurred).	.68

Note: C = child; P = parent; R = responsive.

Source: Compiled by the author.

and/or the total number of ten-second periods during which the parent was in the same room as the child.

2. To reduce the number of variables, sets of conceptually related behaviors were combined.

3. To obtain measures of contingent parental responsiveness, the presence or absence of a parental response to each of the child's expressive behaviors occurring in the same or next ten-second period was tallied and divided by the total number of expressive behaviors observed.

The set of variables thus arrived at are listed and described in Table 6.1.

In addition to making this minute-to-minute quantitative recording, the observers filled out a set of five-point rating scales after the observation hour. These ratings indicate on a more subjective level the observers' judgment of the parents' emotional expresiveness (positive and negative); acceptance of the child's behavior; physical, material, social, and verbal stimulation of the child; responsiveness to the child's distress and demands and to social behavior; and effectiveness of soothing and stimulation. At the end of the study, observers also rated fathers' "availability' from "spends as much time at home as mother" to "spends almost no time with child at home."

Semistructured Situations

Activity Choices

Following the hour of natural observation at the two visits when the children were 15 months old, parents were asked to make a series of choices between pairs of activities to do with the child. The choices were designed to separate social/physical activities (for example, having a pretend tea party, brushing the child's hair, playing "this little piggy") from intellectually stimulating activities (reading a story, playing with a stacking toy, building with blocks) and independent activities (letting children play with the objects by themselves). In order to derive from the simple-choice situation an index of the strength of the parents' preference for these three types of activity, the parent was also asked at the time he or she made each choice to rate from zero to four how easy the choice was. The rationale for doing this was that, if choosing between two activities was very difficult for the parent, the choice should be considered more or less random and not indicative of a real preference for the selected activity, whereas if the choice were easy, that would indicate a clear and strong preference. Two variables were derived from these parental choices: an "intellectual acceleration" score that was the sum of the ease-of-choice ratings for the intellectually stimulating choices and an "independence" score that was the sum of the ease-of-choice ratings for the activities that parents preferred to let children do by themselves.

Assessment of Attachment

After the natural observations at the two visits when the children were 20 months of age, children's attachment to each parent was measured. An identical procedure was followed by the mother at one visit (when the father was not present) and by the father at the other visit (when the mother was in the house but not in the room). It consisted of the following steps: the parent sat at some distance and directed no behavior toward the child for one minute, then looked, smiled, and talked to the child for one minute, called the child to come (one minute), engaged him or her in social interaction (two minutes), and played with a book (four minutes); then the parent left the child (one minute), left the child's room (two minutes), returned (one minute), left the house (two minutes), and returned once more (one minute). The observer, meanwhile, recorded on a checklist for each step of the sequence the child's behavior to the parent (looking at and away, smiling, frowning, vocalizing, gesturing, fretting, crying, touching, affectionately touching, playing, clinging, approaching, avoiding, and staying close or distant). These observed behaviors were combined to form the following variables: negative reaction to parent leaving (frets, cries, clings, gestures, follows), positive reaction to reunion with parent (smiles, vocalizes, touches, affectionately touches, approaches) after separation, physical proximity (approaches, touches, clings, stays close), and social interaction (smiles, vocalizes, affectionately touches, plays) during preseparation episodes. In addition, the observer rated on a five-point scale the child's responsiveness to the parent's social interaction in the attachment situation.

Assessment of Sociability

Immediately following the attachment-to-mother assessment, a friendly but unfamiliar woman came to the house and went through the same sequenced procedure with the child as had the parents. As before, at each step the observer recorded on a checklist the child's social behavior to the adult. The combined frequency of the child's smiling, vocalizing, approaching, affectionately touching, and playing with the stranger was calculated to offer a single overall measure of sociability.

Play Probes

Two parallel "play probes" were carried out following the hour of natural observation at the two consecutive home visits when the children were 30 months old: the first with mother and child only and the second with father, mother, and child. Parents were asked on these occasions to involve the child in a variety of specific play activities: dyadic activities (for example, blowing bubbles, making designs with drinking straws, playing with a toy telephone, reading a book) or triadic activities (playing a game, coloring, throwing or rolling a ball).

Before each dyadic play activity in the second probe when mother and father were both present, children were asked which parent they wanted to do the particular activity with, and that parent played first; then, after a specified length of time, the experimenter asked the child to do the activity with the other parent, and that parent continued the activity for an identical length of time. In addition to recording the child's "preferred" (that is, chosen) parent and the "strength" of that preference (length of time child remained interested, took turns, and did not involve other parent), the observer rated on five-point scales for each play activity the following variables: the parent's ability to engage the child; enjoyment and involvement in the activity; use of the opportunity for social interaction; the teaching style adopted (rewarding, directive); the child's cooperation, enjoyment, and interest in the task and the parent; and the physical distance between parent and child. Ratings on each scale were then combined across play activities (by calculating the mean rating) to evaluate the child's and parents' performance in comparable play activities in three different situations: mother and child alone, mother and child with father present, father and child with mother present.

Daily Records

At each of the three age periods, mothers were asked to fill out a "Baby Day Record" on the day preceding an observation visit. This record consisted of 104 questions about the child's activities from waking until bedtime, questions about what the child did, when, and with whom. For example, for the time immediately after dinner: "Did the baby play? What did he/she play with? Did the baby play with anyone? What did they do together? Did the baby have a bath? Who bathed him/her?" Two variables from these records were calculated for this report: the number of play activities (reading, bedtime routines, excursions, play time) participated in by mother and father and the number of caretaking activities (feeding, bathing, getting up, putting to bed, attending when crying) performed by each.

Attitude Questionnaire

At the 30-month visits each parent was asked to respond to a questionnaire containing three kinds of questions: (1) Nine child-rating scales, on which the parent was asked to rate his or her own child's attractiveness, intelligence, likability, masculinity/femininity, assertiveness, activeness, cooperativeness, and sociability. The purpose of these ratings was to find out whether there were differences between mothers' and fathers' perceptions of their children and, by inference, their attitudes toward their children; (2) An "age-expected" checklist, which was a list of tasks for which parents were asked to indicate the age they expected the child would be able to do each (for example, crossing the street, playing with scissors, going next door alone, using a hammer, taking a bath without help); and (3) An "age-taught" checklist, which was a similar checklist for more intellectual achievements, on which parents were asked to give the age at which they would teach their child each task (for example, counting, naming colors, printing his or her name, reciting the alphabet). For these three questionnaires the measure used in data analyses was the mean value.

Competence Assessments

Finally, one further kind of data was collected: assessment of the child's intellectual and social competence. The Bayley Mental Development Scale was administered by a trained tester at the university to each child at 16 months and again at 22 months. As some of the subjects had already reached the ceiling on the Bayley Mental Scale at 22 months, for the third time period the Minnesota Child Development Inventory (MCDI) was completed by the child's mother. Five separate measures from these tests were analyzed: the Bayley Mental Score at 16 months and 22 months, the MCDI General Development Scale score (a composite score most heavily weighted with conceptual ability and language comprehension and production, and thus roughly comparable to the Bayley Mental Scale), the MCDI Self-Help Scale score (a scale consisting of items like washes face, uses knife, is toilet trained, takes off shoes and socks), and the MCDI Personal-Social Scale score (a social competence measure consisting of items like shows toy to visitor, asks for help, offers to help others, insists on doing by self, apologizes, has a favorite playmate, teases children).

Since intellectual and social competence measures were not collected by nor available to the home observers, these developmental assessments were independent of the data on parents.

Reliability

Three young women served as observers in the study. Interobserver agreement was calculated at the beginning, middle, and end of the observation period of 18 months. Agreement for recording observations was 79 percent over all behaviors on a ten-second interval-by-interval calculation. Reliability of variables from observation to observation, calculated by correlating behaviors between pairs of observations within three weeks of each other, ranged from .27 to .79. Variables showing reliability lower than .42 were dropped from the analysis. Most of the remaining variables had reliability coefficients greater than .60; these reliability coefficients are displayed in Table 6.1.

On rating scales, observers were trained to the point that their judgments were within one scale point of each other; the average reliability between pairs of observations was .71 for ratings. Interobserver agreement for the attachment checklist was over 90 percent.

RESULTS

Children's Behavior to Mother and Father

The first analysis of these data was the comparison of children's behavior with their mothers and fathers. Univariate analyses of variance for repeated measures and correlations between behavior to mother and father were performed for each child measure (skewed variables having first been transformed to logarithms). Data from natural observations were analyzed for each age separately as well as for the means of the three ages combined. Means and F ratios for all significant differences ($p < .10$) that resulted are presented in Table 6.2.

The semistructured assessment of children's attachment to mother and father offered results that were clear and consistent with prior research (see Parke 1979a). When parents' behaviors were specified and controlled in these interaction and separation episodes at 20 months, neither measures of proximity and contact prior to separation nor measures of reaction to separation and reunion differentiated children's attachment relations with mother and father. Children's reunion reactions with mother and father, moreover, were significantly correlated ($r = .76$). Nor was a difference observed in the amount of affiliative interaction (smiling, vocalizing, and playing) with mother versus father in this situation. Only one measure differentiated children's reactions to mother and father in the attachment assessment: children were rated significantly more responsive to play initiated by father than play initiated by mother.

This positive reaction to play with the father was even more clearly differentiated from the reaction to play with mother ten months later when children played with both parents in the triadic "play probe." Children were rated more cooperative, interested, and joyful during play with father in that situation. Eight of the 14 consistently chose to play with father first and displayed a stronger preference for him as playmate.

This preference for play with the father was based on differential quality of play, not quantity, and occurred when parents or children were requested to so interact. In the natural observation, by contrast, in which the amount or frequency of interaction was assessed and no request for play was made, mother was clearly the predominant partner. Differences between children's interaction with mother and father were highly significant when the measure was of the overall amount of interaction. Since these measures were affected by differential opportunity for children to engage in interaction with each parent, however,

TABLE 6.2

Differences in Children's Behavior to Mothers and Fathers

Child Behavior	Mother and Father Present				Mother only Present	
	Mean to Father	Mean to Mother	F Parent	Interaction F Parent by Sex of Child	Mean to Mother	F Father Presence
Natural observations (15, 20, 30 months)						
Looks	0.114	0.221	24.13[a]	4.72[b]		
Vocalizes	0.045	0.125	14.84[c]			
Looks/in room (observation two)	0.201	0.351	5.27[b]			
Vocalizes/in room	0.098	0.215	4.85[b]	4.36[d]		
(observation three, C responsive)	0.028	0.097	7.15[b]			
Touches/in room (observation two)	0.042	0.075	4.61[b]			
Plays/in room (observation one, observation three)	0.036	0.085	4.61[b]	4.56[d]		
Plays R/in room	0.006	0.039	15.37[c]			
Interaction duration	2.600	3.780	5.45[b]			
Play Probes (30 months)						
Cooperation	3.61	1.93	28.36[a]	4.13[d]	3.67	12.08[c]
Enjoyment	3.06	1.93	11.63[c]	6.51[d]	3.06	7.70[b]
Interest in task	3.03	2.04	7.54[b]			
Interest in P	2.65	1.93	2.16[d]	3.42[d]	3.24	6.43[b]
Distance P-C	1.06	1.93	2.95[d]			
Strength of preference	6.25	3.75	4.80[b]			
Attachment assessments (20 months)						
Responsiveness	3.50	2.79	7.41[b]			

[a] $p < .001$.
[b] $p < .05$.
[c] $p < .01$.
[d] $p < .10$.

Note: $df = 1,12$ for all analyses except "in room" measures for mother versus father, in which $df = 1,9$; F = father; C = child; P = parent; R = responsive.

Source: Compiled by the author.

children's behavior was further analyzed as a proportion of the time each parent was in the same room as the child and thus available for interaction. Although the interaction of child with mother was more frequent than that with father in these measures, too, differences were smaller and less consistent as the children grew older. By the time children were 30 months, the only kind of behavior that differentiated between their interactions with mother and father was responsive in nature.

Analyses of variance performed on these data included not only the parents' sex but the child's age and sex, too. No significant interaction of children's behavior toward mother and father with age was observed, but a number of variables interacted with the child's sex. When mother and father were both present, children's preference for playing with father, observed in the play probe, was accounted for entirely by boys, while in the natural observations, in which mother had been observed to be the preferred partner, the difference between behavior to each parent was accounted for largely by girls.

Differences and Similarities between Mothers and Fathers

Analyses of variance for correlated samples were also performed for all parent variables and, in general, revealed differences between mothers and fathers that paralleled those observed for children (see Table 6.3 for all significant differences). The daily records of caretaking episodes performed by each parent clearly demonstrated the predominance of mother in these activities in a typical day. But even during the hours that fathers were at home for the natural observations, mothers were observed to interact more with the children than fathers did, not only in overall amount, but as a proportion of their time in the same room. These differences appeared in all modes of interaction but were more evident in parent-initiated behavior than in responsive parental behavior.

Only one kind of interaction did not differentiate between mother and father in the natural observations. That was social play. No difference was found between mothers and fathers in observed frequency of social play, observers' ratings of the quality of physical or social stimulation, or the proportion of parent-child interaction that was playful. Fathers did not play with children more than mothers, but play was, at least, a kind of interaction—and the only one found here—that was relatively balanced between mother and father, where the father's effort was not "overwhelmed" by the amount of maternal behavior emitted. Play with the father, when it occurred, however, was briefer in duration, more likely to be physically involving, and less apt to be mediated by a toy, and, with boys, it consumed a larger proportion of total parent-child interaction.

Observation of parents' behavior in the play probes adds further information about parental play styles. In the activity choice probe at 15 months, mothers chose activities that were nonsocial and intellectual (usually involving materials), while fathers selected those that were social and physical—thus paralleling the difference in their observed play styles. Later, at 30 months, in the triadic play situation fathers were more likely to direct and reward their children during play and were rated higher than mothers in their ability to engage the child in play. They were particularly able to engage their sons in play and also played with them more in the natural observation: interaction Fs (F1, 12) = 4.12, 3.78, $p < .10$. Daily records kept by the mother offer one further suggestion about the nature of parental play, showing that the father's role as playmate increased over the period from 15 to 30 months.

At the same time as the father was becoming a more frequent playmate, the mother's role as caregiver was diminishing and parents were becoming increasingly undifferentiated on this dimension. This similarity between parents was found for other variables as well. Although the child's interaction with mother was more frequent, it was not more responsive nor was it judged by an observer to be more stimulating, affectionate, or effective. Mothers and fathers did not express different attitudes toward their child on the child rating or age-expected/ age-taught questionnaires. Only the rating of acceptance of the child's behavior differentiated between parents.

Correlational analyses on parental variables revealed other similarities between mothers and fathers. Intercorrelations within the set of observed behavior (ratings and frequencies) for mothers were highly similar to those found for fathers. Only one pattern was distinctly different, and that was related to social play. While positive emotion, physical stimulation, and social play were highly correlated with each other and with other measures of positive interaction with the child for mothers, they were correlated with negative emotion for fathers.

Correlating data over pairs of spouses demonstrated further similarities in mothers' and fathers' behavior—as couples: maternal behavior was significantly correlated with the same kinds of behavior from the father (Table 6.3). The only kinds of behavior that were not significantly correlated between husbands and wives, although they were in a positive direction, were negative behavior and play with objects. For many fathers, these behaviors were never exhibited during the three observations—no father was ever observed to punish his child, for instance—and this may account for the lack of significance in these relations. Generally, pairs of parents were highly similar in terms of the quantity and quality of their interaction with the child.

Correlations between spouses did, however, contain two relations illustrating the differences between maternal and paternal roles. First, parent-initiated physical contact (touches, holds, carries), although positively correlated between mothers and fathers at 30 months ($r = .52$), was negatively correlated earlier at 15 months ($r = -.46$). And second, fathers' social play, although only marginally correlated with the mothers' social play ($r = .50$), was

TABLE 6.3

Differences and Correlations between Mothers' and Fathers' Behavior to Children

Parent Behavior	Mother and Father Present					Mother Only Present	
	Father Mean	Mother Mean	F Parent	Interaction F Parent by Child Age	Correlation Between Father and Mother	Mother Mean	F Father Presence
Natural observations (15, 20, 30 months)							
Physical contact	0.024	0.060	21.74[a]				
Verbal initiation	0.051	0.143	25.09[a]		.77[b]		
Verbal R	0.027	0.077	17.66[b]		.53[c]	0.098	3.44[d]
Verbal positive	0.002	0.016	85.27[a]		.60[c]	0.022	6.94[c]
Verbal/in room	0.151	0.323	6.02[c]		.45[d]	0.346	4.54[c]
Negative behavior	0.004	0.018	11.03[b]				
Plays social	0.015	0.029			.50[d]		
Play object	0.018	0.051	7.59[b]		.76[b]		
Plays/in room	0.062	0.112	4.76[c]		.50[d]		
Social R/in room				4.21[c]			
Observation one	0.031	0.075					
Observation three	0.039	0.036					
Play proportion					.54[c]		
Responsiveness		0.330	4.46[d]	4.59[c]	.53[c]	0.401	11.97[c]
Same room	0.667	0.813			.49[d]		
Observation one	0.560	0.905					
Observation three	0.658	0.670					
Interaction duration	2.600	3.780	5.45[c]		.72[b]		

126

Daily record (15, 20, 30 months)					
Play			3.99[c]		
Record one	1.67	2.58			
Record three	2.00	1.58			
Caretaking	1.78	5.83	121.95[a]	6.98[c]	
Record one	1.25	6.83			
Record three	1.75	4.50			
Play probes (30 months)					
Engages	3.21	2.21	8.35[b]	3.47	.56[c]
Enjoys	2.86	2.21	3.84[d]	3.03	.59[c]
Social interaction		1.50		2.10	.73[b]
Reinforces	1.02	0.43	14.22[b]	1.21	
Directs	1.09	0.61	3.55[d]	1.44	
Observation ratings (15, 20, 30 months)					
Acceptance	3.18	2.79	5.78[c]		
Social stimulation					.63[c]
Verbal stimulation					.53[c]
R to social	2.71	2.72	0.00		.50[d]
Activity choices (15 months)					
Independence	2.07	7.11	6.34[c]		
Intellectual	6.37	10.19	10.13[b]		

Engages 11.39[b]; Enjoys 5.48[c]; Social interaction 5.83[c]; Reinforces 28.54[b]; Directs 13.56[b]

[a] $p < .001$.
[b] $p < .01$.
[c] $p < .05$.
[d] $p < .10$.

Note: $df = 1,12$ for all analyses except "in room" measures for mother versus father, in which $df = 1,9$; F = father; R = responsive.

Source: Compiled by the author.

very highly correlated with mothers' talking ($r = .89$) and playing with the child with toys ($r = .96$). These "cross-modal" correlations, in fact, were the highest coefficients obtained among maternal and paternal variables.

Effect of the Father on Mother-Child Interaction

For all the results described thus far, the data were limited to situations in which mother and father were both present. The possibility that the mother's behavior was affected by the father's presence was explored by comparing maternal behavior in matched pairs of father-present, father-absent observations (Tables 6.2 and 6.3). From these analyses it appeared that there was a significant effect on the mother's behavior of having the father in the house: although maternal behavior in the two situations was correlated (average $r = .52$), the amount of positive and responsive talk by the mother when father was home was significantly less. This was apparently not a by-product of decreased attention to the mother by the child, as contingent maternal responsiveness calculated as a proportion of the child's expressed behaviors revealed the difference even more clearly, and no differences were observed in the frequency of children's behavior to the mother. But merely being "at home" is not the best measure of the father's presence. Therefore, a separate analysis of "in room" behavior was done for those observations during which father was not only home but in the same room as mother and child for more than two-thirds of the observation period (23 observations). This analysis not only replicated the difference in maternal verbal responsiveness but also revealed a significant effect on the amount of mother-initiated play. When father was in the room, mother talked, responded, and played with the child less, $Fs(1,21) = 2.08, 2.59, 2.43, p < .05$.

This same effect showed up when mother and father were requested to play with the child in the play probes (Table 6.3). Mother-child play in the dyadic play situation was significantly greater for every kind of behavior in which a difference between mother and father had been observed in the triadic situation, and, what is more, the amount of social interaction when mother and child were alone was even greater than that of father and child in the triad.

Relations between Parents' Behavior and Child Development

Finally, analyses were carried out to examine associations of maternal and paternal behavior with children's development. This was accomplished by correlating parental variables with measures of children's intellectual ability (Bayley Mental Scale at 16 and 22 months and the MCDI), social competence (MCDI Self-Help and Personal-Social Scales), attachment (positive reaction to reunion with mother and with father), and sociability (interaction with a stranger).

Correlational analyses with intelligence measures (Table 6.4) revealed that, for boys and girls combined, children's intellectual competence was most highly and consistently related to the mother's verbal and materials stimulation, intellectual acceleration, and expression of positive emotion. The paternal variables most closely associated with children's intelligence were the father's engagement of the child in play in the triadic play probe, his positive ratings of the child, his anticipation of the child's independence on the age-expected questionnaire, and the duration of his interactions with the child in the natural observations.

Correlations calculated separately for boys and girls revealed that associations between intellectual ability and mothers' verbal and intellectual stimulation, though significant for the total group, were stronger for girls than for boys. They also revealed this same-sex link between mothers and daughters in correlations of children's intelligence with mothers' positive rating of child, ability to engage child in play, enjoyment of play, and effectiveness of stimulation. With sons, more predictive maternal behaviors all involved physical contact (physical contact, social play, social responsiveness, and negative behavior); predictive paternal variables involved physical and intellectual stimulation (physical stimulation, physical contact, play with objects, intellectual activities choice, and intellectual acceleration in the age-taught questionnaire). Stronger correlations with paternal variables for girls involved primarily positive/verbal interaction (verbal/in room, positive verbal, positive emotion, ability to engage in play, intellectual activities choice [negative], and responsiveness to social behavior).

The next set of analyses performed involved the child's social competence (Table 6.5). The MCDI Self-Help and Personal-Social Scales were found to be related to maternal verbalization and social play and, to a less significant extent, maternal lack of punishment and were reflected in longer mother-child interaction. Mother-son correlations were consistently higher than mother-daughter correlations and more inclusive. Fathers' playful and verbal behaviors, too, were related to children's social competence and reflected in longer interactions (r = .54). In addition, for girls, social competence was correlated with the father's expectation of independence. The most striking sex difference in these correlations, however, involved the parents' expression of positive emotion: for boys, social competence was positively correlated with maternal and paternal warmth, but for girls, it was negatively correlated with these variables.

The third kind of assessment of children's performance was the observation of children's social behavior during interaction with a stranger and after a brief separation from mother or father. These correlations are presented in Table 6.6. For both boys and girls, a positive reaction to reunion with mother was most highly correlated with mother's social responsiveness and father's social play and choice of independent activities; reunion with father was most highly correlated with mother's social responsiveness and father's social stimulation and choice of independent activities.

TABLE 6.4

Correlations between Parental Variables and Children's Intelligence

	Bayley Mental Development Scale (16 months)		Bayley Mental Development Scale (22 months)		Minnesota Child Development Inventory (30 months)	
	Father	Mother	Father	Mother	Father	Mother
Natural observations (15, 20, 30 months)						
Physical contact			.79	.65		
Negative behavior		-.66				
Verbal initiation		.61		.61		.62
Verbal R*			.76			
Verbal positive						
Verbal/in room	.81	.43		.53	.74	.42
Plays social		.60	.79	.74	.65	.84
Plays object			.60			
Plays proportion			.60			
Plays/in room						
Social R*/in room						.65
Same room						
Interaction duration			.60		.50	
Ratings (15, 20, 30 months)						
Positive emotion				.56	.77	.71
Negative emotion						

130

	(1)	(2)	(3)	(4)	(5)
Acceptance	.43				
Physical stimulation	-.79, .48	*.63*			
Social stimulation			.52, .45		
Verbal stimulation	.45	.60	.62	.45	.63
Materials stimulation	.45	*.60*	.69		.49
R* to distress			.46		
R* to social	.80				
Effectiveness			.50		.67
Play probe (30 months)					
Engages		*.50*	.42	.77	.45/.87
Enjoys			.45		.48/.76
Attitudes					
Child rating		*-.65*		.74	-.65/.69
Independence (Questionnaire)	.51				
Acceleration (Questionnaire)	*.69*		.61		
Independence (choices)			.45		
Intellectual (choices)	.77/-.71, .53	67/-.59	.45		.54

*R = responsive.

Note: Underlined correlations are for boys and girls combined; italicized correlations are for boys alone; plain numbers, for girls alone; presented when significance level is different from that for total sample. Table contains all r's $\geq$ .42 (.60, .60); $r_p < .10 = .45$ (.67, .67); $r_p < .05 = .53$ (.75, .75); $r_p < .01 = (.87, .87)$.

Source: Compiled by the author.

TABLE 6.5

Correlations between Parental Variables and Children's Social Competence

	Self-Help		Personal-Social	
	Father	Mother	Father	Mother
Natural observations (15, 20, 30 months)				
Physical contact	.63		.60	
Negative behavior		-.49		
Verbal initiation		.58		
Verbal R*		.72		
Verbal positive				
Verbal/in room	.84	.57		
Play social		.53		.44
Plays object	.51			
Plays proportion	.50			
Plays/in room		.45		
Social R*/in room				.81
Same room				
Interaction duration		.53	.54	.45

Ratings (15, 20, 30 months)

Positive emotion	−.79	*.43/.78*	*.60/−.94*	*.61/−.85*
Negative emotion				
Acceptance	.46			
Physical stimulation		*.46/.88*		
Social stimulation		*.86*		
Verbal stimulation	.51	*.81*	.48	
Materials stimulation	.56	*.47/.78*	.59	.42
R* to distress	.67	*.44/.81*	.52	
R* to social	.55	*.85*	.47	.64
Effectiveness	.61	*.40/.88*	.48	
Play probe (30 months)				
Engages	.51	.44	.73	
Enjoys		*.44*		
Attitudes				
Child rating	.76		.64	.72
Independence (Questionnaire)				
Acceleration (Questionnaire)				
Independence (choices)	−.68			
Intellectual (choices)				*−.76*

* R = responsive.

Note: Underlined correlations are for boys and girls combined; italicized correlations are for boys alone; plain numbers, for girls alone. Table contains all r's ≥ .42 (.60, .60); r_p < .10 = .45 (.67, .67); r_p < .05 = .53 (.75, .75); r_p < .01 = (.87, .87).

Source: Compiled by the author.

TABLE 6.6

Correlations between Parental Variables and Children's Sociability to Parents and Stranger

	Reunion with Mother		Reunion with Father		Interaction with Stranger	
	Father	Mother	Father	Mother	Father	Mother
Natural observations (15, 20, 30 months)						
Physical contact	.51		.91			
Negative behavior	.76			.67	.60	.58
Verbal initiation	.82	.74				
Verbal R*	.75	.83		.86	.65	.43
Verbal positive					.67	
Verbal/in room				.84		.53
Plays social	.78	.59	.47	.81		
Plays object	.60		.84			
Plays proportion			.87	.63		.49
Plays/in room	.70	.61	.62			.44
Social R*/in room	.48	.64	.54	.86		
Same Room	.78		.64		.42	.61
Interaction duration	.78	.59	.89	.57		
Ratings (15, 20, 30 months)						
Positive emotion						.66

134

	1	2	3	4	5	6
Negative emotion						
Acceptance						
Physical stimulation	.45 / *.65*		.66			.59
Social stimulation			.59	.42	.44	.66
Verbal stimulation			*.64*		.44	.72
Materials stimulation						.77
R* to distress		.44				.49
R* to social				.50		.52
Effectiveness						.88
Play probe (30 months)						
Engages						.50
Enjoys						.61
Attitudes						
Child rating					-.59	-.70
Independence (Questionnaire)						
Acceleration (Questionnaire)					.44	
Independence (choices)	.64		.70			
Intelligence (choices)						
Father availability						.71

* R = responsive.

Note: Underlined correlations are for boys and girls combined; italicized correlations are for girls alone; plain numbers, for boys alone; presented when significance level is different from that for total sample. Table contains all *r*'s ≥ $\underline{.42}$ (.60, .60); $r_p < .10 = \underline{.45}$ (.67, .67); $r_p < .05 = \underline{.53}$ (.75, .75); $r_p < .01 = (.87, .87)$.

Source: Compiled by the author.

135

TABLE 6.7

Correlations between Parental Differences and Children's Assessments

Parental Differences	IQ			Self-Help	Personal-Social	Reunion with Mother	Reunion with Father	Sociability
	16 months	22 months	30 months					
Physical contact								
Verbal/in room	.45		.46	.52	.50	.63	.62	.45
Plays in room		.51	.75					
Social R*/in room				.42	.51	.64	.60	-.43
Acceptance (rating)								
Stimulates (rating)	.45	.55		.52				
Enjoys (probe)			-.58	-.43	-.43			
Child rating	-.45	-.50	-.62	-.76				
Independence (Questionnaire)								-.56
Acceleration (Questionnaire)					-.62			.71/-.92
Activity choices	.42	.44	.52	-.74				.95

*R = responsive.

Note: Underlined correlations are for boys and girls combined; italicized correlations are for boys alone; plain numbers, for girls alone; presented when significance level is different from that for total sample. Table contains all r's ≥ .42 (.60,.60); .45 (.67,.67); r_p < .10 = .45 (.67,.67); r_p < .05 = .53 (.75,.75); r_p < .01 = (.87,.87).

Source: Compiled by the author.

The correlations of all parental variables with children's reactions to reunion with parents were higher for boys than for girls and included physical and verbal interaction as well as play and responsiveness. The only significant correlations that were unique to girls were positive correlations of maternal punishment and paternal prominence of play with girls' reunion with father.

Finally, the last kind of developmental assessment analyzed was sociability to a stranger. This kind of behavior for boys and girls was clearly and consistently associated with all kinds of positive maternal behavior in natural observations and play probes. For girls, it was also related to the father's availability and responsible and positive verbalization. For boys, however, sociability with a stranger was associated with the father's negative attitude and behavior.

In addition to correlating children's performance with maternal and paternal behavior separately, a number of difference scores between maternal and paternal behaviors were calculated and correlated with child development measures to assess the effects of parental discrepancies or imbalances (Table 6.7). Differences between parents in amounts of interaction, stimulation ratings, and activity choices were positively related to indexes of children's intellectual and social development. Differences between parents in positive perception of the child and positive involvement in play were negatively related to the child's performance. One sex difference also appeared in these correlations: the discrepancy in parental perceptions of the child was negatively correlated with sociability to a stranger for girls but positively related for boys.

The opposite combination of parental measures—the sums of these parental variables—when correlated with children's performance did not improve predictability over correlations with individual scores of mother or father. To further evaluate the effect of combined parental "input," therefore, a stepwise multiple regression analysis was performed, predicting children's intellectual level from the following variables: verbal interaction, amount of play, negative behavior, time in same room for mother and for father, and father's availability. Maternal variables (verbal and play) entered the regression first, followed by the paternal verbal variable (increasing the coefficient of determination from .55 to .68). The most highly predictive equation in the analysis, $F(5,8) = 13.00, p < .002)$, included all four maternal variables and this single father variable. Inclusion of additional father variables lowered predictability.

Finally, the last analysis of associations between parental variables and child developmental "outcomes" was the examination of changes in parent-child correlations over time. Differences had been documented in the patterns of associations of maternal and paternal behavior with child development. Were there also differences in the directions of those associations? By calculating and comparing the cross-lagged correlations for parental and child behaviors at two time periods, it has been suggested (for example, Crano 1977; Rozelle and Campbell 1969) that the most plausible direction of influence between parents' and children's behavior can be inferred. This manipulation was performed on a set of parental variables and child measures from the present study. Three parental variables were selected for this statistical treatment to illustrate the three central kinds of parent-child interaction: verbal interaction, social play, and object play. These were correlated with assessments of the child's intellectual development that were made within a month of the observation (at 15 and 30 months). Although the 30–month assessment (MCDI) was not the same test as that given at 15 months (Bayley), it was significantly correlated with the Bayley test at 22 months ($r = .63$, $p < .01$) and was thus considered to be a comparable index of the children's intellectual competence. The fact that this measure relied on maternal report is an unfortunate limitation of the analysis.

In the results of the cross-lagged correlational analysis, a consistent difference between mothers and fathers was apparent. The predominant direction of association for mother-child variables was from mother at time one to child at time two. That is, the mother's verbal stimulation and play with toys at 15 months was more closely related to children's intellectual performance at 30 months (for boys, $rs = .63$, $.61$; for girls, $rs = .58$, $.30$) than was children's intellectual performance at 15 months related to maternal verbalization and play at 30 months (for boys, $rs = .10$, $.04$; for girls, $rs = .18$, $.24$). For fathers the pattern of correlations was in the opposite direction; that is, children's intellectual performance at 15 months was associated with subsequent paternal talk and play 15 months later ($rs = .81$ versus $.16$ and $.38$ versus $-.08$ for girls' talk and play and $.33$ versus $-.03$ for boys' play). These directional relations received further support from partial correlation analyses: standardized path coefficients for a two-wave, two-variable model, with the effect of time-one parent or child variables controlled statistically, also suggested that the most plausible direction was from mother to child and child to father.

One further analysis completed the treatment of data in the present study. Cross-lagged correlations between the mother's and father's behavior were also examined for the same three variables. The findings from this analysis showed the father's talking and playing with the child at one age to be highly associated with the mother's talking and playing with the child later (rs from $.55$ to $.89$ compared with rs from $.06$ to $.34$).

DISCUSSION

While definitive empirical conclusions based on this study alone are impossible, because of the small sample size, large number of variables, and exploratory nature of the investigation, the results obtained can generate hypotheses about parental contributions to child development and point the way to further research. Whenever possible, results will be examined in relation to the findings of other investigations.

Of interest are the findings relating to the "affiliative preference" for fathers that has been postulated by Lamb (Chapter 2, this volume). In this study, children were indeed observed to enjoy and cooperate more in play with their fathers than with their mothers. At issue, however, is whether this difference means that children preferred their fathers or merely that they were responding to a more engaging style of interaction on the father's part. The available evidence points to the latter explanation. First, in the attachment situation when mothers' and fathers' behaviors were prescribed and identical, no difference was observed in the frequency of children's affiliative looking, smiling, or vocalizing to mother and father. Second, in the natural observations where maternal behavior was more frequent than paternal behavior, differences in children's affiliative behavior favored mothers, not fathers, and were particularly marked in interaction initiated by the parent rather than the child. Third, analyses of covariance by Belsky (in press b) and Lamb (1977a) demonstrate that covarying out the amount of parental vocalization to the child eliminates differences in children's vocalizations to mother and father. From all this evidence, it seems most likely that differences in the amount of children's affiliative behavior directed to mother and father are a function of the parents' behavior rather than the children's preferences.

Another way of assessing differences in children's preference for mother or father is to examine the quality of children's behavior. This kind of assessment, too, indicates that given a choice between playing with mother or father more children prefer to play with father and that they are more responsive (Lamb, Chapter 2, this volume; attachment situation assessment), cooperative, and involved (triadic play probe) in such play. Only when fathers play, apparently, does children's preferential reaction appear. The implication of this finding, then, is that it is not fathers or even interaction with fathers per se that children prefer but the type of play fathers engage in.

This raises the question, What is the play style that fathers typically adopt? Results of the present study suggest it is a style that the parent also enjoys, one that involves physical proximity and directions and praise for the child; it is social and physical rather than independent and intellectual or based on interaction with objects; it occurs in brief episodes; and it may also be associated with negative affect from the parent. These findings corroborate the results of other investigators who have noted the physically stimulating, rough-and-tumble, nonintellectual nature of paternal play (Lamb, Chapter 2, this volume; Yogman 1977). They also confirm Burlingham's (1973) clinical observation that paternal involvement with the child is more active, exciting, and stimulating than involvement with the mother and, occasionally, also arouses discomfort and anxiety in the child.

The reason this particular style is more typical for fathers than for mothers has yet to be established. We do not know whether it is a function of biological sex differences, cultural expectations, or merely the extent of relative experience mothers and fathers have with their children. One study that investigated this issue by comparing the behavior of mothers and fathers who were either primary or secondary caregivers for their infants found that no matter how extensive fathers' care experience was, they, more than mothers, were likely to play physical games with their infants (Field 1978). This finding rules out relative child-care experience as an explanation for paternal play style. A second finding, that even in monkeys physical play is the primary mode of males interacting with their offspring (Suomi 1977), makes an explanation based solely on cultural role expectations also unlikely.

There seems to be something particularly, perhaps uniquely, masculine in this physical play style—vigorous, abrupt, and sometimes accompanied by negative affect. Perhaps it reflects a socially acceptable and playful form of the more active and aggressive style that characterizes males' social behavior in all cultures and all species (Freedman 1974). This suggestion that fathers' physical play style is biologically based receives further support from another source, the finding in this study and others that paternal play is particularly common and enjoyed with sons. In a laboratory or structured situation, boys have been observed to "spurn" their mothers when their fathers will play (Lamb 1976f; Ban and Lewis 1964; Lynn and Cross 1974), and, while, during observations of natural interaction at home, girls play more with their mothers, boys play significantly more with their fathers (Lytton 1976; Rendina and Dickerscheid 1976). Both findings also occurred in the present study. Finally, prenatally masculinized (androgenized) girls exhibit more rough outdoor play than their hormonally normal sisters (Ehrhardt and Baker 1973). Although this evidence suggests that there may be a biological basis for the distinctive play style of males, it should not be forgotten that this style is supported in our society by cultural expectations for fathers and sons. Parents of boys, even university-educated, more "liberated" parents, believe that mothers' and fathers' roles are different—the mother's role is to be a caregiver and the father's role is to play—and play with sons, all parents agree, can and should be rougher and more physical than play with daughters (Fagot 1974).

In addition to providing evidence about the father's predominant play style, the present study also offered information about the father's play role. Overall, in natural observations when both parents were present, mothers and fathers were observed to play physically with their children in about equal amounts (see also Pedersen, Anderson, and Cain, Chapter 4, this volume; Belsky, Chapter 5, this volume; Fagot 1974; Lamb, Chapter 2, this volume; Smith and Daglish 1977). According to maternal reports, the father's role as playmate was increasing from 15 to 30 months, and more "play periods" in the average day were being engaged in with the father than the mother by the time the children were 2.5 years of age. A further finding of the present study about the father's play role was that fathers who played most with their children physically were married to mothers who talked the most with their children and engaged them in play with objects. Since the latter maternal qualities have been found in other research (Clarke-Stewart 1973) to be central components of "optimal" maternal care, one might infer that the optimal paternal role to go along with effective mothering involves this physical play style. Brody and Axelrad (1978) also found that fathers married to "A" (good) mothers claimed to enjoy their children's company more—perhaps in playful interactions.

The maternal qualities of verbalization and stimulation with objects are not only central in optimal maternal care, they also differentiate mothers' and fathers' interactions with their children. While fathers are more likely to play, mothers' interactions with their children, relative to fathers, are more likely to involve nurturant and caregiving physical contact (see also Belsky, Chapter 5, this volume; Lamb, Chapter 2, this volume; Lytton 1976), stimulation with objects (see also Belsky, Chapter 5, this volume), and conversation (see also Weinraub and Frankel 1977; Golinkoff and Ames 1977; Lytton 1976; Pedersen, Anderson, and Cain, Chapter 4, this volume). This last verbal quality, moreover, has been observed to differentiate men's and women's interactions with children who are not their own (Frisch 1977; Cantor, Wood, and Gelfand 1977). Differences have also been found in how much parents think their children like to be talked to—mothers saying "often," fathers suggesting "sometimes" (Golinkoff and Ames 1977)—and in how tuned in to their children's language parents are—mothers understanding early speech attempts significantly better than fathers (Weist and Kruppe 1977).

Just as males favor physical interaction, verbal exchange may be favored by females. In the present study not only did mothers talk to their children more than fathers, but when both parents were available, girls were particularly likely to direct their vocalizations to their mothers. Although no significant differences were found here in the amount of maternal behavior directed to boys and girls, studies conducted in laboratory settings have reported that mothers address more speech to their daughters (Weinraub and Frankel 1977; Cherry and Lewis 1977) or to unrelated children they believe to be girls (Frisch 1977); since one of these studies (Frisch 1977) controlled for differences in children's behavior by having identical children designated as "boys" or "girls," mother-child differences in verbal interaction are not likely to be simply the result of girls' greater verbal ability and production.

Taken together, then, these studies of parent- and adult-child interaction lay the groundwork for the proposition that there are two biologically based and culturally supported interactive styles—a masculine style involving physical play and a feminine style involving caregiving and conversation. This proposition is further supported by evidence of sex differences in infancy and childhood. When differences between boys and girls have been observed, it is girls who are more sensitive to sound as infants (Bernstein and Jacklin 1973; Watson 1972; Lewis 1978), more verbally productive as infants and toddlers, and more verbally precocious and competent as children and adolescents (see Maccoby and Jacklin 1974). They have been observed to vocalize more to their parents (Weinraub and Lewis 1977; Brooks and Lewis 1974; Messer and Lewis 1972; and the present study). On the other hand, males have been observed, as infants, to be more active and sensitive to physical stimulation (see Lewis 1978; Maccoby and Jacklin 1974), as children, to be more vigorous and active in play with their parents (Maccoby 1972; Smith and Daglish 1977), and to be more likely to engage in rough-and-tumble play (Freedman 1974). Boys spend more time playing (Weinraub and Lewis 1977; McCall 1974; Goldberg and Lewis 1969) and are more often joined in play by their parents (Fagot 1974); children labeled "boys" have been observed to be encouraged in physical activity more often by nonrelated adults (Frisch 1977). In the present study also, boys were rated more active by parents, $F(1,12) = 6.01, p < .05$, and the activities selected by their parents were more often playful, $F(1,12) = 5.30, p < .05$.

Although these studies offer consistent evidence for two biologically sex-linked interaction styles, it is important to note that in adulthood they are not exclusively fixed to males and females; individuals of both biological sexes who were classified by psychological tests as feminine or androgynous have been observed to behave in a nurturant, verbal style with an unfamiliar infant (Bem, Martyna, and Watson 1976). Possibly those classified as androgynous or masculine would exhibit a vigorous physical play style. As sex roles in our society expand and fluctuate, it is especially important to explore such possibilities, studying differences between parents not only as biological males and females but as individuals with preferred interaction styles.

It is also important not to assume that parental roles are permanent and immutable over the lifetime of the child. The importance of the mother's contribution as a physical caregiver has received much attention in discussions of women's rights and roles. In this study, as in others (for example, Kotelchuck 1976; Walker 1972), mothers did more physical caretaking than fathers. But their caregiving role diminished as their children got older. Even in animal studies, maternal nurturance has been observed to decline gradually during the postparturition period (Rosenblatt 1969), and in the present study the decrease in mothers' physical caretaking was also observed. The decrease, moreover, was accompanied by a reversal in the sign of the correlation between maternal and paternal physical contact with the child, from negative at 15 months to positive at 30 months. At 15 months, it seems, if the child was especially attached to the mother and/or the mother especially nurturant to the child, the father had extremely limited physical contact with his offspring. By the time the child reached 2.5 years, however, the father's role as physical caregiver paralleled the mother's.

In highlighting the differences between mothers' and fathers' styles and roles, it is important to place these differences in the broader context of the observed similarities between mothers and fathers such as this one in physical caregiving. In the present study mothers and fathers were also similar in responsiveness, stimulation, affection, and effectiveness, in attitudes about the child, independence, and teaching, and in the patterns of intercorrelations among their behaviors (except for social play). Although fathers appeared to be more accepting of children's behavior (see also Lytton 1976; Fagot 1974), this apparent difference most likely simply reflected the sizable discrepancy between mothers and fathers in overall amount of any kind of interaction with the child rather than a real difference in disciplinary strictness. In general, except in the style of play they adopted, mothers and fathers differed in the amount of time and interaction they had with their children but were relatively similar in the quality of their interaction. Even for behavior that differed in amount, husband and wife pairs were similar (correlated) relative to other parents.

Parent-child interaction can occur in either a dyadic or a triadic situation, and it is interesting to note that, in this study and elsewhere, when both parents were present mothers initiated less talk and play with the children than when they were alone with them (Belsky, in press b; Lamb, Chapter 2, this volume; Pedersen, Anderson, and Cain, Chapter 4, this volume). This finding illustrates the general effect of increasing the number of interactors in a situation (Cleaves and Rosenblatt 1977). But while this may account for the effect of the father's presence on the quantity of maternal behavior, it seems less helpful in accounting for the effect of his presence on the quality of maternal behavior. When the father was present in the situation, the mother was also observed to be less engaging and responsive in her interactions with the child. It is unfortunate that observations of fathers' play with children alone were not made in the study; however, the discrepancy between the quality of mothers' and fathers' play in the triad would still need explanation. Perhaps the discrepancy reflects some tendency on the mother's part to let father—the "playmate"—take "center stage" in such play situations (particularly since in this case she had already "performed" in a similar probe shortly before). At an earlier age (five months), research by Pedersen, Anderson, and Cain (Chapter 4, this volume) shows that the impact of the mother's presence on the father's behavior is the same as the impact of the father's presence on the mother's behavior. The question of whether this reciprocity holds up after the father has become the child's predominant playmate is an open one, however.

The effect of either parent upon the other's interaction with the child becomes especially important as fathers and mothers in this society increasingly share child care responsibilities. With most families (including those in the present study), though, the situation of father alone with young children is relatively uncommon. For this reason, and because the father apparently affects the quality of maternal behavior as well as its quantity, the influence of father on mother may be more important than the reverse. This would fit with the suggestion of previous authors (Lewis and Weinraub 1976) that the father's influence on child development is primarily indirect (mediated by the mother), while the mother's effect is direct.

Evidence for indirect versus direct parental contributions to child development in the present study is provided by analyses of correlations between parental variables and assessments of children's intellectual competence. Patterns of correlations obtained in these analyses suggest that maternal variables associated with intellectual performance, by virtue of their accelerative and stimulating nature, are likely to be influences on the child's intellectual development, while the paternal variables most closely associated with children's intellectual competence—expecting early independence, being able to engage the child in play, rating the child high on competence, and interacting with the child longer—are more likely to be the result of the child's competence. Cross-lagged and partial correlational analyses of parent behavior and children's intellectual competence over time support this view, suggesting that the most plausible causal direction—if such can be inferred—is mother influencing child, child influencing father, and father influencing mother over the time period assessed. Paternal behavior, moreover, did not predict children's IQ as well as maternal behavior did in regression analyses performed on these data; not only did it not affect children's intellectual development, but the amount by which it was exceeded by maternal verbalization, play, and intellectual stimulation was positively related to children's intellectual performance.

Evidence for the first part of this proposed causal chain showing that maternal stimulation and play are linked to children's intellectual development correlationally, and possibly even causally, is available in other research (Clarke-Stewart 1973; McCall, Appelbaum, and Hogarty 1973). Unfortunately, no other studies have looked at causal effects of paternal behavior on children's intellectual development when they have examined correlational links. However, they have generally found associations affected by the child's sex (see Radin 1976). Radin concluded from her review of these studies, in fact, that the most pronounced theme emerging about fathers and their children's intellectual growth is that the bond between fathers and sons is stronger than that between fathers and daughters. She also reported studies showing a parallel same-sex link between mothers and daughters. Results of the present study lend support to this conclusion in regard to parental stimulation, behavior that we have suggested is causally linked to young children's intellectual development. For girls, IQ measures were more strongly associated with mother's verbal and intellectual stimulation; for boys they were related to father's physical and intellectual stimulation. But it may be too simple just to identify a same-sex correlational link; behaviors of mother and father were also correlated with the intellectual performance of their opposite-sexed offspring. In particular, boys' IQs were highly correlated with their mother's physical contact and social-physical play, while girls' IQs were strongly associated with paternal interaction that was social, positive, verbal, and responsive. Here again, this father-daughter correlational pattern gives further evidence that fathers are responding to their children's intellectual performance rather than stimulating it. In the present study, they were responding socially to their more intellectually precocious, verbal, and sociable daughters.*

Although paternal behavior did not appear to influence children's intellectual development in this study, it may have affected their social development. Unfortunately, causal hypothesis testing was not possible for this domain, since social variables were each assessed at only one age. Children's social competence, measured by the MCDI and reflected in long interactions with both mother and father, was found to be related to verbal interaction and play with both parents. Relations between social competence and these particular parental behaviors have not been explored in previous research, but other correlations with social competence found in the present study are supported in studies of children's autonomy. In this study and observations by Baumrind and Black (1967), boys were autonomous when mother and father were both warm and affectionate. For girls, however, the opposite relation occurred: they were independent and socially competent when mother and father were less warm and when father expected independence at a young age (see also Nakamura and Rogers 1969). Baumrind and Black suggest that girls need more "tension" to develop autonomy, while for boys, since autonomy is part of their traditional role, parents can be warmer. Our results do not permit assignment of causal direction to this relation between children's autonomy and parental warmth, but if this explanation is true, it should also be noted that too much tension—from maternal punishment—has a negative effect on social competence for both boys and girls.

Another measure of children's social development was the assessment of their reaction to reunion with each parent after a brief separation. A positive reunion with both mother and father was related to maternal responsiveness and paternal social play. The latter quality, which we have found to be a central component of paternal behavior, was not related to intellectual or social competence, then, but—what could be less surprising—to children's joy at seeing their father after a brief separation. Other research, both observational and experimental, supports this finding, suggesting that children's social behavior with their fathers is influenced by the father's involvement and play (Kotelchuck 1976; Pedersen and Robson 1969; Zelazo et al. 1977). What is surprising is that the effect was revealed even more clearly in children's reunions with their

---

*Girls exceeded boys on measures of IQ, $F = 4.79$, $p < .05$; vocalization, F at 30 months $= 5.96$, $p < .05$; cooperation, enjoyment, and interest, F s $= 11.20$, $p < .01$; 4.36, $p < .06$; 5.45, $p < .05$ in the play probe. Their fathers were better able to engage them in play—$F = 8.92$, $p < .01$—and interact with them effectively, $F = .394$, $p < .07$ (df $= 1,12$ for all comparisons).

mothers. Only when fathers' social play was combined with negative maternal behavior was the reunion with father and not with mother predicted from paternal variables (for girls). The reverse relation was demonstrated for children's sociability with a stranger: sociability was related to positive interaction with mother and negative paternal behavior (for boys). Boys who were particularly friendly to a female stranger, it seems, may have been so as a result of experience with a female at home that was not only positive but saliently so in its contrast with the father's behavior. Girls apparently did not need such contrast; they were more positive to the stranger when both parents were positive and interactive.

What these findings seem to suggest is that the father's contribution to children's development lies particularly in the social-affective domain. It does not appear that the father makes a contribution to the child's intellectual development over and above that of the mother at this early age (especially for daughters), but he does appear to be an important source of social stimulation. He plays with his children in a particularly enjoyable and engaging way and relieves his wife from being engulfed with constant child care and contact; he facilitates the development of social competence in his daughter and sociability in his son. Perhaps most important of all, he fosters affectionate interaction among all members of the family.

7

OVERVIEW: ANSWERS AND REFORMULATED QUESTIONS

Frank A. Pedersen

Integration of the great number of results from these investigations is a challenge because of their diversity. Not only were questions formulated in varied ways, but differences in methodology—subjects, measures, and analytical strategies—are also apparent. What is important, then, is whether useful conclusions are possible. Is the array of statistical results anything more than a Rorschach inkblot that, in the process of its interpretation, betrays more about personal attitudes, values, and ideologies than about objective descriptions of experience? The reader is invited to organize his or her own conclusions with the hope that there is some convergence in our interpretations.

First, an evaluative perspective is suggested. The investigations share a common imperfection: each is long on variables and short on subjects. This limitation, plus the practice of making multiple statistical tests on the same data corpus, increases the risk of repeated Type I errors (Larzelere and Mulaik 1977; Hays 1973). The most hopeful possibility in this situation is to look for replication of findings across independent investigations. Findings that appear in two independent studies at merely the 10 percent level of confidence have a combined probability of occurring by chance only 1 percent of the time. Even if replication at a precise operational level does not occur, conceptually congruent findings are worthy of greater confidence. Within such a framework, this chapter will review briefly some of the findings that appear more reliable, raise important issues, and suggest future directions. The goal is to sharpen the focus of our present understanding of early experience in the family setting.

BASES FOR COMPARING RESULTS

Features that contribute to the samples being relatively homogeneous provide bases for the most meaningtul comparisons of results. The findings reported in this volume, after all, reflect the roles, behaviors, and attitudes prevalent in the five samples of families that were studied. Among the characteristics that each sample shared are the following:

1. The families were, of course, two-parent, the structure that represents 80 percent of U.S. households with children under 18 years of age (Glick and Norton 1977). The special circumstances of the single-parent father or other less prevalent family structures were not considered.
2. Virtually all families were white and living in middle-class socioeconomic circumstances. The United States' ethnic minorities and the socioeconomically disadvantaged were not included. The range of cultural variation in family roles as well as other distinctive features of early experience were therefore reduced.
3. Although attitudes and values regarding the family were likely to be flexible in many cases, most families maintained a traditional, differentiated role organization. The fathers assumed principal responsibility for providing the economic resources for the family. The mothers, as a group, were the primary caregivers for the children during the period when the fathers were out of the home and associated with their employment. When both parents were with the child, each family's own variety of role specialization or sharing prevailed.
4. The investigations were completed within a relatively narrow historical period, extending from 1972 (Clarke-Stewart) to 1978 (Belsky). Major secular changes are unlikely to have occurred in attitudes and behavior in regard to children and family roles, "cohort effects" which have been identified over longer time spans.

It is also important to appreciate that there were several important differences in the investigations, differences that either may make comparisons difficult or be responsible for seemingly inconsistent results. One is that a principal control variable in each investigation was the age of the child. Three investigations overlapped with each other at age 15 months (Lamb, Belsky, and Clarke-Stewart), but two studies involved infants at earlier age periods. As a consequence, inferences about changes in family experience associated with different maturity levels of the child must be traced across, rather than within, samples. A second difference is that, among the two samples of young infants, one consisted totally of bottle-fed infants (Parke and Sawin) and one was predominantly breast-fed (Pedersen, Anderson, and Cain). Comparisons of the samples and previous research on feeding practices show that there are important socioeconomic correlates of this decision (more breast-fed infants are found now among higher socioeconomic level (SES) families) and that the father's behavior is a factor in the decision (Switzky, Vietze, and Switzky 1979). Finally, the observational methodologies had some variation, which means that each investigation contained some variables not found in others, and there were some differences in the situations that were observed.

OVERVIEW OF FINDINGS

Parental Similarities and Differences

What can be said regarding the general questions posed in Chapter 1? To begin, what are the similarities and the differences that fathers and mothers show in their interaction with infants and toddlers? When parents were observed in relatively similar situations, an important qualification to be sure, most of the studies showed more variables on which mothers and fathers were indistinguishable from each other than variables on which they were different. Parke and Sawin analyzed 27 variables derived from two different situations, feeding and play. Although there was variation at different age periods, only three variables consistently differentiated mothers and fathers. Pedersen, Anderson, and Cain found, at age five months, that 3 out of 12 variables distinguished mothers and fathers. Belsky reported, at age 15 months, that 2 out of 13 variables were significantly different. Lamb focused more upon the infant's behavior toward the parents than the reverse, especially in the early series of his observations. Even so, in his measures of types of play and the reasons for which parents held infants, approximately two-thirds of all comparisons were not significantly different. Only Clarke-Stewart's findings indicated a greater proportion of measures distinguishing mothers and fathers than was the case in other investigations. One reason for this apparent inconsistency is that she employed multiple measures of verbalizations to the child, each of which differentiated mothers and fathers. While the measures emphasized qualitatively different components of verbal interaction, at a different level of abstraction they may be seen as multiple markers of the single finding that mothers talk more to children than do fathers. On balance, there is rather high concordance among the investigations that maternal and paternal behaviors have more areas of similarity than difference.

If one may metaphorically consider the variables examined as various threads of experience from which human relationships are woven, it is clear that in most important respects the parent-infant relationship is neither distinctly maternal nor paternal. The social responses linking parent and child are more unique to the human species than a gender classification of parent. Stated in another way, mothers and fathers may be seen as having certain hierarchies of responses available with which to relate to children; in spite of individual variation, undoubtedly affected by past experiences with children and selective sensitivities, attitudes, values, and socialization goals, there is generally as great a variation between different mothers or different fathers as there is between mothers and fathers as separate groups. In one respect this finding is all the more remarkable because it occurred in families with rather differentiated roles. As Field (1978) has shown, even greater similarity occurs when mothers and fathers have more similar experience with infants in their day-to-day lives.

Each investigation also contained variables on which mothers and fathers were significantly different. An important question is whether there was any degree of constancy in these differences. Clearly, replication of results did occur. First, in these samples, the mother more often than the father was involved in meeting the physical caregiving needs of the child. This was true, of course, during her extended periods of sole responsibility for the child, which the father did not experience. More important, even in the periods when both parents were available to interact with the child or when the structure of the observations controlled for the duration of each parent's time with the child, the mothers spent more time in caregiving activities. Allowing for variation in measures, it is striking that every investigation found mothers more likely to assume caregiving activities. While Fine (1976) and Russell (1978) have identified families that give expression to an ideology in which the father shares more equally in caregiving during the periods he is with the child, their number in these samples obviously did not affect the more general picture of the mother having greater caregiving responsibility.

The interpretation as to why mothers tend to perform more caregiving activities is entirely problematic. One view emphasizes the special biological "connectedness" of mother and child, first through pregnancy and childbirth and then nursing (Lewis and Weinraub 1976). Opposing the sociobiological tradition, sociologists (compare Oakley 1972) have argued that child care needs tend to be met on the basis of social roles that, in present cultural circumstances, have virtually no biological constraints. An empirical resolution does not appear possible on a matter so deeply influenced by personal values.

Since the mother is more frequently the caregiver, is the father-child relationship unique because the father and child are so often partners in play? Here the findings appear equally clear: mothers and fathers were generally equally likely to engage the child in playful episodes. When differences occurred, they were in regard to quality of play. Two studies (Belsky; Pedersen, Anderson, and Cain) found no differences between mothers and fathers on several measures of duration of play. Clarke-Stewart found that the father's play role was prominent, relative to the mother's, only in the situation that gave him special support or incentive—the "play probe," in which he was asked by the investigator to play with the child. Parke and Sawin found but one measure of playful social stimulation—mimicking the child's facial expression—that occurred more often by fathers. Finally, Lamb's several measures of types of play clearly indicated that it was style, not quantity, that differentiated mothers and fathers.

The stylistic difference that distinguished parents was well described in Clarke-Stewart's discussion of her findings: the fathers' play more often involved physical handling, rapid or unpredictable behavior, and the quick release of stimuli; mothers' play styles appeared more often to be verbal and perhaps didactic. Clarke-Stewart advanced the idea that these patterns, while culturally supported, may have a strong biological basis, echoing Margaret Mead's (1949,

p. 170) hypothesis that the musculature in males favors frequent changes in activity and more vigorous responses versus repetitive, more modulated activities for females. Lest this generalization appear unequivocal, some negative evidence also must be appreciated. Parke and Sawin and Belsky did not report consistent parental differences in physical handling, while Pedersen, Anderson, and Cain found that the father's proclivity to engage in physically robust interactions occurred only in three-person situations.

Other areas in which parental differences occurred, corroborated by independent investigations, include verbalizations and smiling. Mothers appear to interact verbally with children more frequently than do fathers. Pedersen, Anderson, and Cain reported this with preverbal five-month-old infants, while Clarke-Stewart, with toddlers, found on four different measures that mothers verbalized more than fathers. Further support for this proposition is found in Fagot's (1974) observations of 12 toddlers in the home and in Rebelsky and Hank's (1971) investigation of 10 infants, based on tape recordings of parental verbalizations. Again, Clarke-Stewart's integrative discussion can hardly be added to, except to note that there are also some negative findings (Belsky; Parke and Sawin; Field 1978).

Smiling toward infants also appeared more prevalent among mothers in the two investigations that explicitly examined this variable (Parke and Sawin; Pedersen, Anderson, and Cain) as well as other research (Field 1978; Parke and O'Leary 1976; Parke, O'Leary, and West 1972). All of these investigations were with very young infants.

Finally, there is one area of behavior in which the findings were unanimously contrary to a cultural stereotype, even though one study disagreed with the other two. No investigation (relevant only in the toddler groups) showed fathers more frequently than mothers to be the disciplinarian, concerned with limit setting or punishing undesired behavior. Clarke-Stewart found that mothers more frequently administered negative sanctions (in keeping with their greater involvement generally), while Lamb's analyses of the reasons for physical contact between parent and child indicated that mothers more often than fathers disciplined the child. Belsky found no difference between mothers and fathers in restrictive behavior, perhaps because his sample of toddlers was younger than in the other two and, therefore, controls were less frequent by both parents. In any case, the sterotypic image of father as disciplinarian is without empirical support, and, with young children, the weight of the evidence is that mothers more frequently are restrictive. These findings are further invalidation of the Freudian model of early experience, which portrays the father as the more severe disciplinarian.

The next major question is how the child's age or sex affects parental behaviors. First, caregiving behavior clearly decreases as the child matures. Since this is an area in which the mother initially is salient, developmental change is in the direction of greater similarity between mother and father.

Another certain generalization is that there are no main effects for the sex of the child on parental behavior. This means that, in whatever way mothers and fathers may have differentiated boys and girls, they never did it in the same way. This too is important in the light of previous findings of differential treatment by mothers of their own male or female infants (Moss, Robson, and Pedersen 1969; Lewis 1978; Weinraub and Frankel 1977; Cherry and Lewis 1977) as well as differential treatment by mothers of infants (not their own) labeled as "boys" or "girls" (Frisch 1977; Smith and Lloyd 1978; Will, Self, and Datan 1976).* The findings in this volume—an absence of main effects for gender of infant on parental behavior—mean that differential maternal behaviors toward males and females are often offset by the father's opposite or reciprocal patterns. In some cases, this effect was strong enough to show up as a statistical interaction of sex of parent by sex of infant on parental behavior. Limiting studies of sex typing to maternal behavior clearly gives an incomplete picture of early experience.

Looking across the ages spanned in several investigations, the possibility occurs that statistical interactions involving sex of parent and sex of infant follow a U-shaped frequency distribution. Five interactions were prevalent in Parke's and Sawin's sample in early infancy. At age five months, however, Pedersen, Anderson, and Cain reported that they found fewer interactions than would be expected by chance. Interactions of this nature were also infrequent in Belsky's data at age 15 months. Lamb reported that in regard to play styles, a sex of parent by sex of infant interaction was not evident in the first year of life but did emerge clearly in the second year. Similarly, supporting her data in the toddler period, Clarke-Stewart presented evidence from several sources that mothers and fathers treat sons and daughters differentially, partly in response to differential sensitivities in children as well as sex-linked behavioral tendencies in the parents. Thus a hypothesis may be advanced that mothers and fathers first are selectively responsive to the sex of the child during early infancy, perhaps a period when sex-typing stereotypes are strong because experience with the child is also relatively limited. Subsequently, they may be somewhat less differentiating on the basis of sex through the first year of life as they acquire more experience with their child's individuality. Then differential treatment may emerge more clearly in the second year, a period when behavioral differences between male and female children are also more apparent. This hypothesis is precarious, of course, because it involves generalizing between studies rather than within longer-term longitudinal samples.

As to the precise nature of interactions involving sex of parent and sex of infant, one pattern appears consistently: stimulating behaviors occur more

---

*Fathers were not included in any of these investigations.

prominently in same-sex pairs of parent and infant. Minor variations on this general theme were found by Parke and Sawin; Belsky; Lamb; and Clarke-Stewart. Clarke-Stewart, moreover, further delineated the nature of stimulation modality preferences, hypothesizing a verbal-physical dichotomy that favors, respectively, female and male parent-infant pairs. Although she suggested a biological basis for such differences, others (compare Hoffman 1977) have argued that differential treatment of the sexes is socially determined and likely to become less evident over the years. In contrast, affectionate behavior was reported to occur more frequently in opposite-sex pairs by Parke and Sawin and in same-sex pairs by Belsky. Thus no consistency is apparent in this area.

The Infant's Behavior

An important theoretical issue, articulated especially by Lamb, is whether infants form attachment relationships with both parents. Although traditional indexes of attachment (for example, the infant crying at separation from an attachment figure) do not become apparent until the second half of the first year, it is likely that the basis of an attachment relationship—reciprocal responsiveness—begins much earlier. There are several findings regarding early reciprocity in Parke's and Sawin's investigation; these findings also have implications for subsequent attachment relationships. Although not replicated in different investigations (because no one else examined the problem), a basic pattern in reciprocity was identified that was replicated with multiple behaviors: from birth to three months, both parent and infant show progressively greater temporal coordination of each's behavior with the other. This pattern, moreover, is basically similar with father and mother. The findings suggest that the underlying basis of attachment relationships, mutual sensitivity to and coordination of behavior with another, emerges quite early and shows a similar developmental course with father and mother.

Both Lamb and Clarke-Stewart presented findings that, at later ages, infants establish attachment relationships with both parents. These results confirm other findings that infants typically form multiple attachment relationships consistently with responsive and stimulating adults (Schaffer and Emerson 1964; Ainsworth 1963; Marvin et al. 1977). In spite of diverse criteria for defining attachment, this conclusion appears unequivocal.

Lamb especially emphasized that the father-infant and mother-infant attachment relationships are nonredundant because of the distinctive experiences provided by the father. A slightly more qualified conclusion is that the father-infant attachment relationship has some nonredundant elements, but there are also many ways in which mothers and fathers behave similarly with children and evoke similar behavior from children. Undoubtedly qualitative variation also occurs in the father-infant attachment relationship. Just as

Ainsworth et al. (1971) identified multiple categories for describing mother-infant attachment—albeit in rather evaluative terms—it would seem important to identify multiple patterns of father-infant attachments in both descriptive and dynamic understandings that recognize the spectrum of variation found in the family today. Lamb's findings, for example, suggest that there may be certain developmental periods when, if the infant experiences stress, differential attachment behavior occurs and other periods when mothers and fathers appear equally satisfactory sources of comfort. Such findings imply that changes or transformations occur in the nature of the father-infant attachment relationship, but little else is known regarding these changes.

Findings regarding another major component of behavior directed toward parents—affiliative responses—also show rather consistent results. Affiliative behaviors—smiling, laughter, looking, and vocalizations—are highly refractive to rates and levels of stimulation emitted by the interactive partner. Thus, the affiliative preferences that children often show toward their fathers, as reported by Lamb and Clarke-Stewart, appear to be largely a function of the activating and engaging style of behavior with which fathers relate to their children. In addition to responding with affiliative behavior because of the father's social initiations, elsewhere (Pedersen et al. 1979) the speculation was advanced that fathers may have a strong "novelty effect," which may intensify reciprocal responsiveness. The father's briefer periods of availability may provide a contrast with the extended periods of interaction the child has experienced with the mother, thus increasing the salience of his behavior. Heightened affiliative responsiveness would be expected to occur. That infants and toddlers are responsive to social novelty would explain why, in Lamb's finding, in some cases more affiliative behavior was directed to the visitor than to the mother.

The Husband-Wife Relationship

One of the most consistent findings to emerge from this set of investigations is the effect of the presence of one parent on the other parent's interaction with the child. Rates of behavior consistently diminish when another person enters the interactive context, a finding reported in three investigations: Lamb; Pederson, Anderson, and Cain; and Clarke-Stewart. The same effect occurred when the parent was interacting with infant or toddler, and father and mother influenced each other similarly. This result appears different from effects observed in the hospital setting with newborn infants (Parke and O'Leary 1976), where the presence of the spouse enhanced affective responsiveness. The psychological significance of diminished interaction rates should be considered. Pedersen, Anderson, and Cain emphasized the ecological significance of this finding; traditional family role organization determines that much of the father's interaction with the infant occurs in three-person settings. This may have the effect of reducing overall rates of behavior between father and infant compared to the more prolonged periods in dyadic contexts that mother and infant characteristically experience. Perhaps the father's tendency to engage in interludes of more intense and arousing bouts of focused play with the infant may be a paradoxical response to the "pull" toward diminished rates of interaction characteristic of three-person settings. This hypothesis would explain why in two investigations (Lamb; Pedersen, Anderson, and Cain) the father's robust interactions with the infant were observed principally in three-person settings.

Analyses also show that in three-person settings behaviors between parent and infant are coordinated or synchronized with spouse interactions. The infant experiences less stimulation of a focused nature during periods when mother and father are in active communication with each other. Moreover, the infant appears capable of monitoring its own behavior in relation to the changes that the parents exhibit, indicating that rather complex learning opportunities occur that are unique to social settings larger than dyadic units. It is also clear that conflicting needs for social interaction may readily occur in three-person (or larger) settings, since focused interaction between two partners requires coordination of behavior with interaction involving a third.

The above findings may be seen as structural influences upon parents and infant. Less is known about psychological dynamics, which may affect relationships among family members. Since most socialization research has been formulated in terms of dyadic parent-child units, the psychological influences of one or more other persons have been examined infrequently. These complex influences may be one of the greatest conceptual and methodological challenges to our understanding of early experience in the family.

Developmental Outcomes

One of the core research problems in developmental psychology is the identification of experiential determinants of the child's cognitive and social development. The more definitive research literature on this problem is dominated by studies of maternal influences, as there have been no long-term investigations of paternal behavior. The studies by Belsky and Clarke-Stewart are truly pioneering efforts because they contain descriptions of maternal and paternal behavior as well as appraisals of the infant's developmental status. Cross-comparisons of results are not meaningful, however, because neither investigation employed the same outcome measures. The direction of influence (whether parental behavior socialized the infant's competence, or vice versa) among family members is ambiguous in Belsky's cross-sectional study, as he readily acknowledged; and Clarke-Stewart's small sample precluded definitive findings, even though her longitudinal design lends itself more readily to causal inferences. Thus "hard" evidence on so important a problem is lacking. Without falling back on scientific nihilism and such shibboleths as "more research is needed," what meaningful conclusions can be drawn? There are several.

Both investigations reported a network of statistical associations connecting paternal behavior and the child's development. There were more correlations that were significant than would be expected by chance, and the patterning of findings lent itself to conceptually coherent explanations. Thus, the status of the research problem has been advanced beyond mere exhortation that "fathers are important" to the delineation of specific associations and the identification of psychological processes that may affect development.

The data suggest further that both paternal and maternal associations with children in early development are selective. Leaving aside the question of direction of influence for the moment, findings are consistent with the proposition that neither parent is an exclusive determinant for all spheres of the child's development. Clarke-Stewart suggested that maternal influences figure more prominently in the child's cognitive attachment as measured by the Bayley Mental Development Scales and the Minnesota Child Development Inventory. These findings are plausible in that the mothers provided more verbal stimulation and the tests involved language mastery. Paternal influences appeared more prominently in measures of social competence and were related to social and affective stimulation. A further selective factor was reported by Clarke-Stewart: there were suggestions that effects were often sex-linked, with more clear-cut associations occurring between same-sex parent and infant pairs.* Belsky, utilizing exploratory competence as the outcome measure, found more correlations that were significant in paternal rather than maternal behavior. The father's verbal and affective stimulation were both associated with competence in the child's play. Thus it appears that each parent makes differential contributions in varied spheres of the child's development.

Finally, Belsky and Clarke-Stewart highlighted the necessity of formulating more complex statistical and analytic strategies for evaluating joint parental influences. Belsky, concentrating on contemporaneous influences, experimented with configurational approaches to parental behavior. By classifying parents above or below the median on one or more variables, he generated various family constellations that were significantly associated with different levels of exploratory conpetence. His analytic strategy showed meaningful findings that would have been obscured by traditional approaches of corre-

---

*If environmental influences reliably occur more strongly in same-sex parent and infant pairs, this fact would contradict a different hypothesis regarding environmental influences that was developed by investigation of maternal behavior alone. Moss (1974) and Yang and Moss (1978) have argued that female infants are responsive to environmental influence (by the mother), but male infants are not. It is clear that the inclusion of data on fathers may alter some very fundamental notions of how psychological development occurs.

lating parental behavior and child outcome. For example, restrictive behavior, which was not correlated significantly with exploratory competence for either mothers or fathers, did show a significant negative association when families in which both parents were restrictive were identified. A strategy that preserved the family as the unit of analysis was more sensitive than analyses that treated mothers and fathers merely as separate socialization influences.

Clarke-Stewart focused on sequential influences. By employing cross-lag correlational analyses, she suggested that mothers directly influenced the child's development; the father's responsiveness to the child's cognitive competence, in turn, appeared to foster further maternal involvement at a later period. She proposed a model of chains of influence over time; Belsky proposed contemporaneous patterning of influences. Logically, each's formulation can be extended to incorporate the other's idea as well. This would produce a mind-boggling picture of various patterns of maternal and paternal behavior, which are modified or transformed over time—reactively or causally—in relation to the child's development. Such a system perspective pushes the concept of psychological causation well beyond primitive notions of unidirectional influences.

NEW DIRECTIONS

In the process of addressing the core questions of this volume, these investigations contributed to uncovering new issues and reformulating old questions. Problems have been illuminated that were not so apparent when researchers in developmental psychology were content to examine early experience in more fragmented units. These are matters that are likely to be the agenda of future research, but sensitivity to them will also assist the interpretation of data that are now available. In the section that follows, propositions will be presented that were developed from considering the results of the five investigations and other relevant research findings.

"Paternal Behavior" Is Not a Unitary Phenomenon

An analysis performed in each investigation was to dichotomize the sample of parents on the basis of their biological gender, thus comparing mothers and fathers. This provided information that could not have been known any other way, and the comparisons appeared meaningful because virtually all of the families maintained relatively traditional roles. At the same time, this research strategy did not illuminate the full diversity of family adaptations that might exist within a traditional schema. Present research findings on fathers and the literature on psychological androgyny suggest that it may be more meaningful to partition the sample of fathers into at least two subgroups based on the prominence of their caregiving activities. In more extreme expression, some fathers have assumed the primary caregiver role (Field 1978; Mendes 1976) or adopted work-sharing employment patterns that permit more extended time with children (Grønseth 1975). Even with traditional work role assignments, a significant proportion of men—perhaps 25 percent in U.S. samples—appear to participate actively in caregiving during the time they are with the child (Fine 1976; Kotelchuck 1976). Because this pattern is qualitatively different from more general normative findings, it appears useful to distinguish this group from fathers for whom caregiving is a secondary component of their paternal role.

It also appears that variation in fathers' caregiving rates may be identified in distinctive family patterns. For example, Fine (1976) noted that "nontraditional" fathers are often—but not always—married to women who have highly salient career commitments. Russell (1978) found associations between the father's caregiving behavior and a measure of psychological androgyny, which he then related to different patterns of maternal sex role identification. By differentiating fathers according to the prominence of their caregiving behavior and classifying mothers along other conceptually relevant dimensions, configurational approaches to analyzing experience in the family are possible. This strategy, in keeping with Belsky's analyses, should highlight patterns of early experience that are presently obscured when mothers and fathers are thought of only as globally different classes of parents. Parenthetically, while the father for whom caregiving is prominent may be described as androgynous or feminine in sex-role identification, there may be other bases for the same behavior. Thus, it is not necessarily helpful to anchor family patterns to personality constructs. Merely attaching a label to behavior does not automatically increase our understanding of it (Fisk 1978). What is important is that experience is described in a sufficiently differentiated manner so that its effects can be evaluated. Realizing that there is substantial variation in paternal behavior in different families is the first stage in this process.

The Psychological Dynamics and Process of Second-Order Effects Warrant Greater Attention

The expansion of our understanding of early experience from a dyadic mother-and-infant unit to a three-person family system has highlighted a major new problem: understanding how interactions between two people influence and are influenced by a third person. In particular, the husband-wife relationship, the component of the family in which developmental psychology has shown relatively little interest, is brought into sharp focus. Evidence of its importance for parenting roles is available largely in sociological research literature, which rarely includes detailed examination of parent-infant interaction, and in a few investigations that have attempted to bridge disciplinary boundaries.

Investigation of the "transition to parenthood" indicates that the marital relationship is intertwined with the experience of crisis as well as gratifications associated with the birth of a child (Russell 1974). Russell found, inter alia, that planning the baby's conception, conceiving after marriage rather than before, and the number of months the parents were married before parenthood were related to the experience of gratifications at parenthood. Her interpretation of the data emphasized communication between parents as a factor that facilitated the transition to parenthood for both mother and father. A similar theme relating communicative effectiveness in the marital unit to both paternal and maternal competence was reported by Heath (1976).

Other research linking the husband-wife and parent-infant relationships has emphasized the concept of emotional support, particularly from the husband to the wife to maintain effective mother-infant interaction. Adaptation in feeding appears facilitated by the father's encouragement and positive evaluation of the mother (Pedersen 1975; Price 1977; Switzky, Vietze, and Switzky 1979). Feiring and Taylor (in press) found that the mother's evaluation that there were supportive elements in her relationship with the "secondary parent" was associated with her provision of stimulation to the baby and a heightened sensitivity to infant signals. Depressive symptoms in the postpartum period have been related retrospectively to emotionally cold and distant husbands (Kaplan and Blackman 1969) and, in one prospective investigation, to marriages with a high degree of husband-wife role segregation (Oakley 1979). Taken together, these findings suggest that it is the expressive elements in the father's relationship with his wife that contribute strongly to the wife's morale and sense of competence as a mother.

It is also interesting to speculate whether fathers need emotional support to maintain effective parent-infant relationships. Fein and Apfel (1976) reported that many men feel excluded and "left out" after the birth of a child; they also feel that there are few institutional supports for the paternal role. There has been little research on fathers' needs for support, perhaps because traditional sex-role stereotypes foster the image of men as "strong" and women as "weak" and in greater need of support.

While the marital relationships may have supportive functions in relation to parenting, it is also likely that the child's behavior or characteristics may impinge on the marital relationship. For example, Leifer et al. (1972) reported anecdotally that in families where there was a childbirth complication (that is, prematurity) there was a disproportionate stress upon the marital relationship. More divorces occurred during the follow-up period in families where there was a premature childbirth than in the control group of full-term infants. The implication of the findings is that difficulties in coping with the child heightened tension and conflict in the marital relationship. Other findings within the normal range indicate that the perception of the infant as "quiet" (eats well, easily adapts to routines, sleeps through the night, and so on) is related to less of a sense of crisis in the initial stages of parenthood (Russell 1974). Thus, second-order effects may be conceptualized in terms of any family member upon any other relationship and vice versa. Understanding the psychological bases for such effects was not the major focus of the investigations in this volume, but it is an important task for future research.

Family Experiences Should Be Traced in a Developmental Perspective

The controversial psychiatrist and family therapist, R. D. Laing, proposed that families should be understood within a developmental perspective (1969, p. 77). He lamented that we can study directly only a minute slice of the family chain: "What patterns can we hope to find, when we are restricted to [study] only three out of at least 4,000 generations?"

A more modest goal is merely to trace family experiences through pregnancy into a child's second or third year of life. There are a number of reasons why such time boundaries are likely to have a favorable yield of information in relation to the investment of research resources. First, the husband-wife relationship might be appraised prior to experience with the child. By the conventional practice of dating developmental events in terms of the child's age, it is easy to forget that the marital relationship has its own developmental history. Since husbands and wives may differ in their "readiness" to make the role transition to parenthood, this factor may affect their subsequent role performance. Appraisal of the marital relationship after the birth of the child is hopelessly confounded by the influence of the child's unique characteristics, the birth circumstances, and current experience with the child.

A second reason for a developmental perspective is so that patterns of parental and child behavior may be traced more comprehensively. Parke's and Sawin's findings revealed that mothers and fathers often change relative to each other, suggesting that each learns from the other as well as adapts to the child. Since their investigation was the only one to provide such data, little is known regarding the consistency of the patterns. The course of the child's attachment relationships with mother and father may also be plotted, and differential patterns may be identified; no investigation has traced the father-infant relationship from a preattachment period to the time when focused relationships are clearly manifest. The tasks of parenthood also change with the child's developmental progress. Time spent in caregiving activities diminishes over time; concern with socialization goals, both cognitive and social, increase over time, even as the child's emergent autonomy expresses itself. The efficacy with which each parent adapts to these new developmental levels may impinge upon the marital relationship, a factor that may explain findings of change in marital satisfaction associated with different ages of the child (Rollins and Galligan

1978). The selective influence of sex of parent and sex of child also has a developmental course. Only a few inferences were possible from the present set of investigations in regard to these processes.

Finally, a developmental perspective will permit stronger inferences regarding causal factors that selectively influence varied spheres of the child's development. As noted previously, there is but scant information regarding the joint influence of mothers and fathers on development. By tracing development into the second or third year, it is also likely that reliable criterion measures may be utilized that, on the basis of other research findings, are known to be reasonably predictive of longer-term development.

The Data of Early Experience Should Include Cognitive Constructions, Beliefs, and Values

The investigations in this volume placed a premium on objective description of parental and child behavior. Except for a few questionnaire measures, there was little attention paid to parental beliefs or attitudes that accompany or undergird behavior. Disinterest in this type of information is characteristic of psychologists' reaction against self-report methods, which are often held in low esteem as sources of valid information regarding environmental experience. As Parke and Sawin cogently argued, however, this reaction may represent some confusion regarding what verbal report is and is not. Clearly, it is not a substitute for independent observation of behavior; verbal report taps the subject's cognitive constructions of his or her own behavior or that of another and the goals, values, and expectations that a person holds for self or another. Since there is variation in how behavior is apprehended and responded to, one explanation of these differences is in terms of individual perceptions and interpretations.

To illustrate the significance of varied interpretations of behavior, the infant's cry is a good case in point. The cry has high demand character, but its "meaning" may be conceived of as an effort at communication, an assertion of willfulness and power, a relatively random event, or a rebuke toward the parent. In addition, one's own role definition and the definition held for one's partner are likely to influence the posture taken toward the infant's cry. Moreover, parents may have different expectations about the consequence of their responses to the infant's cry. There is a spectrum of beliefs ranging from the view that prompt attentiveness "spoils" the baby to the view that communication is enhanced. These conceptions of self and other influence both the initiation of and response to behavior; they also provide a broader basis for understanding otherwise naked responses. Unless the investigator attempts to see the world through the research participant's eyes, there is a great temptation to impose only one's own constructions upon descriptive findings.

A second reason to broaden the data of early experience is to recognize that communication among family members occurs at different levels. Many, though not all, spouse interactions involve exchanges at the level of verbal constructions. The content or meaning in communication is a major component affecting the course of interaction.* Before the child acquires well-developed symbolic capacities, however, interaction is primarily in terms of more concrete sensory events. Since family communication occurs at these varied levels, research methodologies should be used that are sensitive to different levels of experience. Description at one level alone is likely to result in an incomplete characterization of family interactional processes.

Finally, consideration of data at the level of verbal expression in combination with other behavioral levels is likely to highlight some interesting inconsistencies that affect family functioning. For example, Goode (1970, p. 21) has suggested that middle-class parents often are highly equalitarian in their ideology regarding men's and women's roles, but, at another level, the man's commitment to his business or professional career exerts a preemptive influence on many family decisions. Working-class men may hold to an ideology of masculine dominance, but in the day-to-day functioning of the family the wife/mother is more likely to have relative equality, if not actual domination, in many spheres. Inconsistencies between what is articulated verbally and what occurs at other behavioral levels should be understood as part of the ways in which families function. Neither level alone is what is "real." But by excluding beliefs, ideology, or other verbal constructions of experience, psychologists are restricting themselves to only part of the data concerning family interactional processes.

A FINAL WORD

Researchers of early development for a long period have been asking very complex questions in oversimplified forms. Perhaps the major contribution of the five investigations in this volume is to highlight the complexity of early experience when it is viewed in the perspective of a family system. Data have been presented that document the similar and distinctive experiences provided by mother and father. In addition to effects of the larger family role organization, the ongoing relationship between parents influences the child's experiences. The child responds selectively to each parent, determined, in part, by how each behaves and by the child's own sensitivities and temperamental characteristics. Parents jointly influence different spheres of development, effects that are

---

*Perhaps this is why researchers of the marital relationship often rely only on methods that address cognitive constructions of experience.

the product of complex patterns of experience, and each is responsive to the child's emerging social and cognitive competence. There is a developmental course that undergirds and modifies these ongoing processes. In short, a comprehensive view of early experience must involve new research designs, different variables, and more complex analytic strategies than we have been content with in the past. This conclusion does not mean that there is no place for highly focused investigations of selected aspects of environment-organism interaction. It does mean, however, that the findings of such research cannot be mistaken for comprehensive statements of early experience. Fictions of convenience that have been serviceable in the past will have to be replaced by more ambitious attempts to conceptualize a broader range of environmental experience and more complex notions of psychological influence.

BIBLIOGRAPHY

Abelin, E. L. The role of the father in the separation-individuation process. In J. B. McDevitt & C. F. Settlage (Eds.), *Separation-individuation*. New York: International Universities Press, 1971.

Abelin, E. L. Some further observations and comments on the earliest role of the father. *International Journal of Psychoanalysis*, 1975, *56*, 293–302.

Ainsworth, M. D. The effects of maternal deprivation: A review of findings and controversy in the context of research strategy. In *Deprivation of maternal care: A reassessment of its effects*. Geneva: World Health Organization, 1962.

Ainsworth, M. D. The development of infant-mother interaction among the Ghanda. In B. M. Foss (Ed.), *Determinants of infant behavior* (Vol. 2). London: Methuen, 1963.

Ainsworth, M. D. Patterns of attachment behavior shown by the infant in interaction with his mother. *Merrill-Palmer Quarterly*, 1964, *10*, 51–58.

Ainsworth, M. D. Object relations, dependency, and attachment: A theoretical review of the infant-mother relationship. *Child Development*, 1969, *40*, 696–1025.

Ainsworth, M. D. Attachment and dependency: A comparison. In J. L. Gewirtz (Ed.), *Attachment and dependency*. Washington D.C.: Winston, 1972.

Ainsworth, M. D. The development of infant-mother attachment. In B. M. Caldwell & H. N. Ricciuti (Eds.), *Review of child development research III*. Chicago: University of Chicago Press, 1973.

Ainsworth, M. D., & Bell, S. M. Attachment, exploration and separation: Illustrated by the behavior of one-year-olds in a strange situation. *Child Development*, 1970, *41*, 49–67.

Ainsworth, M. D., Bell, S. M., & Stayton, D. J. Individual differences in strange situation behavior of one-year-olds. In H. R. Schaffer (Ed.), *The origins of human social relations*. New York: Academic, 1971.

Aldous, J. Family interaction patterns. *Annual Review of Sociology*, 1977, *3*, 105–135.

Aries, P. *Centuries of childhood: A social history of family life*. New York: Vintage, 1962.

Bakon, D. *The duality of human existence*. Chicago: Rand McNally, 1966.

Balswick, J. O., & Peck, C. W. The inexpressive male: A tragedy of American society. *Family Coordinator*, 1971, *20*, 363–368.

Ban, P. L., & Lewis, M. Mothers and fathers, girls and boys: Attachment behavior in the one-year-old. *Merrill-Palmer Quarterly*, 1964, *22*, 195–204.

Baumrind, D., & Black, A. E. Socialization practices associated with dimensions of competence in preschool boys and girls. *Child Development*, 1967, *38*, 291–327.

Beckwith, L. Relationships between attributes of mothers and their infants' I.Q. scores. *Child Development*, 1971, *42*, 1083–1097.

Bell, R. Q. A reinterpretation of the direction of effects in studies of socialization. *Psychological Review*, 1968, *75*, 81–95.

Bell, S. M. The development of the concept of the object as related to infant-mother attachment. *Child Development*, 1970, *41*, 291–311.

Belsky, J. Mother-infant interaction in the home and laboratory: The effect of setting. Paper presented at the biennial meeting of the Society for Research in Child Development, New Orleans, 1977.

Belsky, J. The interrelation of parental and spousal behavior during infancy in traditional nuclear families: An exploratory analysis. *Journal of Marriage and the Family*, in press. (a)

Belsky, J. Mother-father-infant interaction: A naturalistic observational study. *Developmental Psychology*, in press. (b)

Bem, S. L. The measurement of psychological androgyny. *Journal of Consulting and Clinical Psychology*, 1974, *42*, 155–162.

Bem, S. L., Martyna, W., & Watson, C. Sex typing and androgyny: Further explorations of the expressive domain. *Journal of Personality and Social Psychology*, 1976, *34*, 1016–1023.

Berman, P. W. Social context as a determinant of sex differences in adults' attraction to infants. *Developmental Psychology*, 1976, *12*, 365–366.

Bernard, J. *The future of motherhood*. New York: Penguin, 1975.

Bernstein, R. C., & Jacklin, C. N. The 3½-month-old infant: Stability of behavior, sex differences, and longitudinal findings. Unpublished master's thesis, Stanford University, 1973.

Biller, H. B. *Father, child, and sex-role*. Lexington, Mass.: Heath, 1971.

Biller, H. B. *Paternal deprivation: Family, school, sexuality, and society*. Lexington, Mass.: Heath, 1974.

Biller, H. B. The father and personality development: Paternal deprivation and sex-role development. In M. E. Lamb (Ed.), *The role of the father in child development*. New York: Wiley, 1976.

Block, J. H. Conceptions of sex role: Some cross-cultural and longitudinal perspectives. *American Psychologist*, 1973, *28*, 512–526.

Bowlby, J. *Maternal care and mental health*. Geneva: World Health Organization, 1951.

Bowlby, J. *Attachment and loss, I: Attachment*. New York: Basic Books, 1969.

Bowlby, J. *Attachment and loss, II: Separation: Anxiety and anger*. New York: Basic Books, 1973.

Bradley, R. A. *Husband-coached childbirth*. New York: Harper & Row, 1965.

Brazelton, T. B., Tronick, E., Adamson, L., Als, H., & Wise, S. Early mother-infant reciprocity. In M. A. Hofer (Ed.), *Parent-infant interaction*. Amsterdam: Elsevier, 1975.

Bretherton, I., & Ainsworth, M. D. Responses of one-year-olds to a stranger in a strange situation. In M. Lewis & L. A. Roseblaum (Eds.), *The origins of fear*. New York: Wiley, 1974.

Brody, S., & Axelrad, S. *Mothers, fathers, and children: Explorations in the formation of character in the first seven years*. New York: International Universities Press, 1978.

Bronfenbrenner, U. The changing American child: A speculative analysis. *Journal of Social Issues*, 1961, *17*, 6–18. (a)

Bronfenbrenner, U. Some familial antecedents of responsibility and leadership in adolescents. In L. Petrullo & B. Bass (Eds.), *Leadership and interpersonal behavior*. New York: Holt, Rinehart and Winston, 1961. (b)

Bronfenbrenner, U. Developmental research, public policy and the ecology of childhood. *Child Development*, 1974, *45*, 1–5. (a)

Bronfenbrenner, U. *Is early intervention effective?* Department of Health, Education and Welfare Publication No. (OHD) 76-30025, Washington, D.C., 1974. (b)

Bronfenbrenner, U. Toward an experimental ecology of human development. *American Psychologist*, 1977, *32*, 513–531.

Bronson, W. Early antecedents of emotional expressiveness and reactivity control. *Child Development*, 1966, *37*, 793–810.

Brooks, J., & Lewis, M. Attachment behavior in thirteen-month-old, opposite-sex twins. *Child Development*, 1974, *45*, 243–247.

Brown, D. G. Sex role preference in young children. *Psychological Monographs*, 1956, *70*, 1–19.

Brown, D. G. Masculinity-femininity development in children. *Journal of Consulting Psychology*, 1957, *21*, 197–203.

Brown, D. G. Sex role development in a changing culture. *Psychological Bulletin*, 1958, *55*, 232–242.

Burlingham, D. The preoedipal infant-father relationship. *Psychoanalytic Study of the Child*, 1973, *28*, 23–47.

Cairns, R. B., & Green, J. A. How to assess personality and social patterns: Observations or ratings? In R. B. Cairns (Ed.), *The analysis of social interactions: Methods, issues and illustrations*. Hillsdale, N.J.: Erlbaum, 1979.

Caldwell, B. M. The effects of infant care. In M. L. Hoffman & L. W. Hoffman (Eds.), *Review of child development research* (Vol. 1). New York: Russell Sage Foundation, 1964.

Cantor, N. L., Wood, D. D., & Gelfand, D. M. Effects of responsiveness and sex of children on adult males' behavior. *Child Development*, 1977, *48*, 1426–1430.

Carew, J., Chan, I., & Halfar, C. Observed intellectual competence and tested intelligence: Their roots in the young child's transactions with his environment. Paper presented at the biennial meeting of the Society for Research in Child Development, Denver, 1975.

Casler, L. Perceptual deprivation in institutional settings. In G. Newton & S. Levine (Eds.), *Early experience and behavior*. Springfield, Ill.: Charles C. Thomas, 1968.

Charlesworth, W. Human intelligence as adaptation: An ethological approach. In L. B. Resnick (Ed.), *The nature of intelligence*. Hillsdale, N. J.: Erlbaum, 1975.

Cherry, L., & Lewis, M. Differential socialization of girls and boys: Implications for sex differences in language development. In C. Snow & N. Waterson (Eds.), *Development of communication: Social and pragmatic factors in language acquisition*. New York: Wiley, 1977.

Clarke-Stewart, K. A. Interactions between mothers and their young children: Characteristics and consequences. *Monographs of the Society for Research in Child Development*, 1973, *38* (6–7, Serial No. 153).

Clarke-Stewart, K. A. *Child care in the family: A review of research and some propositions for policy*. New York: Academic Press, 1977.

Cleaves, W. T., & Rosenblatt, P. C. Intimacy between adults and children in public places. Paper presented at the meetings of the Society for Research in Child Development, New Orleans, March 1977.

Cohen, L. J., & Campos, J. J. Father, mother, and stranger as elicitors of attachment behaviors in infancy. *Developmental Psychology*, 1974, *10*, 146–154.

Cook, A. H. *The working mother: A survey of problems and programs in nine countries.* Ithaca: Cornell University, 1978.

Crano, W. D. What do infant mental tests test? A cross-lagged panel analysis of selected data from the Berkeley growth study. *Child Development*, 1977, *48*, 144–151.

Decarie, T. G. *Intelligence and affectivity.* New York: International Universities Press, 1965.

Dick-Read, G. *Childbirth without fear* (2nd ed.). New York: Harper & Row, 1965.

Ehrhardt, A. A., & Baker, S. W. Hormonal aberrations and their implications for the understanding of normal sex differentiation. Paper presented at the meetings of the Society for Research in Child Development, Philadelphia, March 1973.

Epstein, A. S., & Radin, N. Motivational components related to father behavior and cognitive functioning in preschoolers. *Child Development*, 1975, *46*, 831–839.

Erikson, E. *Childhood and society.* New York: Norton, 1950.

Fagot, B. J. Sex differences in toddlers' behavior and parental reaction. *Developmental Psychology*, 1974, *10*, 554–558.

Fein, G., & Apfel, N. The development of play: Style, structure and situations. Unpublished manuscript, 1976 (available from authors, Merrill-Palmer Institute, Detroit, Michigan).

Feiring, C., & Taylor, J. The influence of the infant and secondary parent on maternal behavior: Toward a social systems view of infant attachment. *Merrill-Palmer Quarterly*, in press.

Feldman, S., & Ingham, M. Attachment behavior: A validation study in two age groups. *Child Development*, 1975, *46*, 319–330.

Fenson, L., Kagan, J., Kearsley, R., & Zelazo, P. The developmental progression of manipulative play in the first two years. *Child Development*, 1976, *47*, 232–236.

Ferguson, C. A. Baby talk in six languages. *American Anthropologist*, 1964, *66*, 103–114.

Field, T. Interaction behaviors of primary versus secondary caretaker fathers. *Developmental Psychology*, 1978, *14*, 183–184.

Fine, R. A. Men's entrance to parenthood. *Family Coordinator*, 1976, *25*, 341–348.

Fisk, D. W. *Strategies for personality research.* San Francisco: Jossey-Bass, 1978.

Forrest, T. The paternal roots of male character development. *The Psychoanalytic Review*, 1967, *54*, 81–99.

Freedman, D. G. *Human infancy: An evolutionary perspective.* Hillsdale, N.J.: Erlbaum, 1974.

Freud, S. *An outline of psychoanalysis.* New York: Norton, 1948.

Frisch, H. L. Sex stereotypes in adult-infant play. *Child Development*, 1977, *48*, 1671–1675.

Gewirtz, H. B., & Gewirtz, J. L. Visiting and caretaking patterns for kibbutz infants: Age and sex trends. *American Journal of Orthopsychiatry*, 1968, *38*, 427–443.

Gewirtz, J. L. (Ed.). *Attachment and dependency*. Washington, D.C.: Winston, 1972.

Ginsburg, H., & Koslowski, B. Cognitive development. *Annual Review of Psychology*, 1976, *27*, 29–61.

Glick, P. C., & Norton, A. J. Marrying, divorcing, and living together in the U.S. today. *Population Bulletin*, 1977, *32*, (5), 3–39.

Goldberg, S., & Lewis, M. Play behavior in year-old infants: Early sex differences. *Child Development*, 1969, *40*, 299–311.

Golinkoff, R. M., & Ames, G. J. Do fathers use "motherese"? Paper presented at the meetings of the Society for Research in Child Development, New Orleans, March 1977.

Goode, W. J. *World revolution and family patterns*. New York: Free Press, 1970.

Goodenough, E. W. Interest in persons as an aspect of sex differences in the early years. *Genetic Psychology Monographs*, 1957, *55*, 287–323.

Gottman, J. Time series analysis of continuous data in dyads. In M. E. Lamb, S. J. Suomi, & G. R. Stephenson (Eds.), *Social interactional analysis: Methodological issues*. Madison: University of Wisconsin Press, 1979.

Gottman, J. M., & Bakeman, R. The sequential analysis of observational data. In M. E. Lamb, S. J. Suomi, & G. R. Stephenson (Eds.), *Social interactional analysis: Methodological issues*. Madison: University of Wisconsin Press, 1979.

Graves, Z. R., & Glick, J. The effect of context on mother-child interaction: A progress report. *Quarterly Newsletters of the Institute for Comparative Human Development*, 1978, *2*, 41–46.

Greenberg, M., & Morris, N. Engrossment: The newborn's impact upon the father. *American Journal of Orthopsychiatry*, 1974, *44*, 520–531.

Grønseth, E. Work-sharing families: Adaptations of pioneering families with husband and wife in part-time employment. *Acta Sociologica*, 1975, *18*, 202–221.

Haith, M., & Campos, J. Human infancy. *Annual Review of Psychology*, 1977, *28*, 251–293.

Harlow, H. F. The nature of love. *American Psychologist*, 1958, *13*, 673–685.

Hartup, W. W. Levels of analysis in the study of social interaction: An historical perspective. In M. E. Lamb, S. J. Suomi, & G. R. Stephenson (Eds.), *Social interactional analysis: Methodological issues*. Madison: University of Wisconsin Press, 1979.

Hays, W. L. *Statistics for the social sciences* (2nd ed.). New York: Holt, Rinehart and Winston, 1973.

Heath, D. H. Competent fathers: Their personalities and marriages. *Human Development*, 1976, *19*, 26–39.

Hebb, D. O. *The organization of behavior*. New York: Wiley, 1949.

Heilbrun, A. B., Jr. An empirical test of the modeling theory of sex-role learning. *Child Development*, 1965, *36*, 789–799.

Heilbrun, A. B., Jr. Measurement of masculine and feminine sex-role identities as independent dimensions. *Journal of Consulting and Clinical Psychology*, 1976, *44*, 183–190.

Herzog, E., & Sudia, C. Children in fatherless families. In B. M. Caldwell and H. N. Ricciuti (Eds.), *Review of child development research* (Vol. 3). Chicago: University of Chicago Press, 1973.

Hess, E. H. Ethology and developmental psychology. In P. H. Mussen (Ed.), *Carmichael's manual of child psychology* (3rd ed.). New York: Wiley, 1970.

Hetherington, E. M., & Deur, J. L. The effects of father absence on child development. *Young Children*, 1971, *26*, 233–248.

Hill, R. Contemporary developments in family theory. *Journal of Marriage and the Family*, 1966, *28*, 10–26.

Hinde, R. A. On describing relationships. *Journal of Child Psychology and Psychiatry*, 1976, *17*, 1–19.

Hinde, R. A., & Atkinson, S. Assessing the role of social partners in maintaining mutual proximity as exemplified by mother-infant relations in rhesus monkeys. *Animal Behaviour*, 1970, *18*, 169–176.

Hinde, R. A., & Spencer-Booth, Y. The behavior of socially living rhesus monkeys in their first two and a half years. *Animal Behaviour*, 1967, *15*, 169–196.

Hoffman, L. W. Changes in family roles, socialization, and sex differences. *American Psychologist*, 1977, *32*, 644–657.

Hoffman, M. Power assertion by the parent and its impact on the child. *Child Development*, 1960, *31*, 129–143.

Honzik, M. Environmental correlates of mental growth: Prediction from a family setting of 21 months. *Child Development*, 1967, *38*, 337–364.

Hunt, J. McV. *Intelligence and experience*. New York: Ronald Press, 1961.

Inhelder, B., Lezine, I., Sinclair, H., & Stambak, M. Les debuts de la function symbolique. *Archives de Psychologie*, 1972, *41*, 182–243.

Johnson, M. M. Sex role learning in the nuclear family. *Child Development*, 1963, *34*, 315–333.

Kaplan, E. H., & Blackman, L. H. The husband's role in psychiatric illness associated with childbearing. *Psychiatric Quarterly*, 1969, *43*, 396–409.

Keller, H. R., Montgomery, B., Moss, J., Sharp, J., & Wheeler, J. Differential parental effects among one-year-old infants in a stranger and separation situation. Paper presented at the meetings of the Society for Research in Child Development, Denver, April 1975.

Kessen, W., & Fein, G. Variation in home based infant education: Language, play and social development. Final report to the Office of Child Development, Department of Health, Education and Welfare, August 1975.

Kitzinger, S. *The experience of childbirth*. Baltimore: Penguin, 1972.

Klaus, M. H., & Kennell, J. H. *Parent-infant bonding*. St. Louis: Mosby, 1976.

Kotelchuck, M. *The nature of the child's tie to his father*. Unpublished doctoral dissertation, Harvard University, 1972.

Kotelchuck, M. The infant's relationship to the father: Experimental evidence. In M. E. Lamb (Ed.), *The role of the father in child development*. New York: Wiley, 1976.

Kotelchuck, M., Zelazo, P., Kagan, J., & Spelke, E. Infant reaction to parental separation when left with familiar and unfamiliar adults. *Journal of Genetic Psychology*, 1975, *126*, 255–262.

Laing, R. D. *The politics of the family*. New York: Penguin, 1969.

Lamaze, F. *Painless childbirth*. Translated by J. R. Celestin. Chicago: Henry Regenery, 1970.

Lamb, M. E. Fathers: Forgotten contributors to child development. *Human Development*, 1975, *18*, 245–266. (a)

Lamb, M. E. *The relationships between infants and their mothers and fathers*. Unpublished doctoral dissertation, Yale University, 1975. (b)

Lamb, M. E. Effects of stress and cohort on mother- and father-infant interaction. *Developmental Psychology*, 1976, *12*, 435–443. (a)

Lamb, M. E. Interactions between eight-month-old children and their fathers and mothers. In M. E. Lamb (Ed.), *The role of the father in child development*. New York: Wiley, 1976. (b)

Lamb, M. E. Interactions between two-year-olds and their mothers and fathers. *Psychological Reports*, 1976, *38*, 447–450. (c)

Lamb, M. E. The one-year-old's interaction with its parents. Paper presented to the Eastern Psychological Association, New York, April 1976. (d)

Lamb, M. E. Parent-infant interaction in eight-month-olds. *Child Psychiatry and Human Development*, 1976, *7*, 56–63. (e)

Lamb, M. E. The role of the father: An overview. In M. E. Lamb (Ed.), *The role of the father in child development*. New York: Wiley, 1976. (f)

Lamb, M. E. Twelve-month-olds and their parents: Interaction in a laboratory playroom. *Developmental Psychology*, 1976, *12*, 237–244. (g)

Lamb, M. E. The development of mother-infant and father-infant attachments in the second year of life. *Developmental Psychology*, 1977, *13*, 637–648. (a)

Lamb, M. E. The development of parental preferences in the first two years of life. *Sex Roles*, 1977, *3*, 495–497. (b)

Lamb, M. E. Father-infant and mother-infant interaction in the first year of life. *Child Development*, 1977, *48*, 167–181. (c)

Lamb, M. E. The effects of parent-parent on infant-parent interaction. Unpublished manuscript (submitted for publication), 1978. (a)

Lamb, M. E. The effects of the social context on dyadic social interaction. In M. E. Lamb, S. J. Suomi, & G. R. Stephenson (Eds.), *Social interaction analysis: Methodological issues*. Madison: University of Wisconsin Press, 1978. (b)

Lamb, M. E. Infant social cognition and "second order" effects. *Infant Behavior and Development*, 1978, *1*, 1–10. (c)

Lamb, M. E. Social interaction in infancy and the development of personality. In M. E. Lamb (Ed.), *Social and personality development*. New York: Holt, Rinehart and Winston, 1978. (d)

Lambie, D., Bond, J., & Weikart, D. *Home teaching with mothers and infants*. Ypsilanti, Michigan: High/Scope Educational Research Foundation, 1974.

Lansky, L. M. The family structure also affects the model: Sex role attitudes in parents of preschool children. *Merrill-Palmer Quarterly*, 1967, *13*, 139–150.

Larzelere, R. E., & Mulaik, S. A. Single-sample tests for many correlations. *Psychological Bulletin*, 1977, *34*, 557–569.

Leifer, A. D., Leiderman, P. H., Barnett, C. R., & Williams, J. A. Effects of mother-infant separation on maternal attachment behavior. *Child Development*, 1972, *43*, 1203–1218.

Lerner, R., & Spanier, G. (Eds.). *Child influences on marital and family interaction: A life-span perspective*. New York: Academic Press, 1978.

Levenstein, P. Cognitive growth in preschoolers through verbal interaction with mothers. *American Journal of Orthopsychiatry*, 1970, *40*, 426–432.

Lewis, M. (Ed.). *Origins of intelligence*. New York: Plenum Press, 1976.

Lewis, M. Sex stereotypic behavior in infants: An analysis of social-interpersonal relationship. Princeton, N.J.: Educational Testing Service, 1978. (ERIC Document Service No. ED 057 904).

Lewis, M., & Goldberg, S. Perceptual-cognitive development in infancy: A generalized expectancy model as a function of the mother-infant relationship. *Merrill-Palmer Quarterly*, 1969, *15*, 81–100.

Lewis, M., & Rosenblum, L. A. (Eds.). *The origins of behavior* (Vol. 1). *The effect of the infant on its caregiver*. New York: Wiley, 1974.

Lewis, M., & Weinraub, M. Sex of parent X sex of child: Socioemotional development. In R. C. Friedman, R. M. Richart, & R. L. Van de Wiele (Eds.), *Sex differences in behavior*. New York: Wiley, 1974.

Lewis, M., & Weinraub, M. The father's role in the infant's social network. In M. E. Lamb (Ed.), *The role of the father in child development*. New York: Wiley, 1976.

Lind, R. Observations after delivery of communications between mother-infant-father. Paper presented at the International Congress of Pediatrics, Buenos Aires, October 1974.

Lowe, M. Trends in the development of representational play in infants from one to three years: An observational study. *Journal of Child Psychology and Psychiatry*, 1975, *16*, 33–47.

Lynn, D. B. *The father: His role in child development*. Monterey: Brooks/Cole, 1974.

Lynn, D. B., & Cross, A. R. Parent preference of preschool children. *Journal of Marriage and the Family*, 1974, *36*, 555–559.

Lytton, H. Comparative yield of three data sources in the study of parent-child interaction. *Merrill-Palmer Quarterly*, 1974, *20*, 53–64.

Lytton, H. The socialization of two-year-old boys: Ecological findings. *Journal of Child Psychology and Psychiatry*, 1976, *17*, 287–304.

Maccoby, E. E. Differential socialization of boys and girls. Paper presented at the annual convention of the American Psychological Association, Hawaii, September 1972.

Maccoby, E. E., & Jacklin, C. N. *The psychology of sex differences*. Stanford: Stanford University Press, 1974.

Marvin, R., VanDevender, T., Iwanoga, M., LeVine, S., & LeVine, R. Infant-caregiver attachment among the Hausa of Nigeria. In H. McGurk (Ed.), *Ecological factors in human development*. Amsterdam: North-Holland, 1977.

McCall, R. B. Exploratory manipulation and play in the human infant. *Monographs of the Society for Research in Child Development*, 1974, *39* (2, Serial No. 155).

McCall, R. B., Appelbaum, M. I., & Hogarty, P. S. Developmental changes in mental performance. *Monographs of the Society for Research in Child Development*, 1973, *38*, (3, Serial No. 150).

Mead, M. *Male and female*. New York: Morrow, 1949.

Mendes, H. A. Single fathers. *Family Coordinator*, 1976, *25*, 439–444.

Messer, S. B., & Lewis, M. Social class and sex differences in the attachment and play behavior of the one-year-old infant. *Merrill-Palmer Quarterly*, 1972, *18*, 295–306.

Mischel, W. Sex typing and socialization. In P. H. Mussen (Ed.), *Manual of child psychology* (Vol. 2). New York: Wiley, 1970.

Money, J., & Ehrhardt, A. A. *Man and woman, boy and girl*. Baltimore: Johns Hopkins University Press, 1972.

Moss, H. A. Early sex differences and mother–infant interactions. In R. C. Friedman, R. M. Richart, & R. L. Van de Wiele (Eds.), *Sex differences in behavior*. New York: Wiley, 1974.

Moss, H. A., Robson, K. S., & Pedersen, F. A. Determinants of maternal stimulation of infants and consequences of treatment for later reactions to strangers. *Developmental Psychology*, 1969, *1*, 239–246.

Nakamura, C. Y., & Rogers, M. M. Parents' expectations of autonomous behavior and children's autonomy. *Developmental Psychology*, 1969, *1*, 613–617.

Oakley, A. *Sex, gender and society*. London: Maurice Temple Smith, 1972.

Oakley, A. *Housewife*. New York: Penguin, 1976.

Oakley, A. *Becoming a mother*. Oxford, England: Martin Robertson, 1979.

Olsen, D. H. The measurement of family power by self-report and behavioral methods. *Journal of Marriage and the Family*, 1969, *17*, 545–550.

Orlansky, H. Infant care and personality. *Psychological Bulletin*, 1949, *46*, 1–48.

Orne, M. T. On the social psychology of the psychological experiment: With particular reference to demand characteristics and their implications. *American Psychologist*, 1962, *17*, 776–783.

Orthner, D., Brown, T., & Ferguson, D. Single-parent fatherhood: An emerging life style. *Family Coordinator*, 1976, *25*, 429-438.

Parke, R. D. Social cues, social control and ecological validity. *Merrill-Palmer Quarterly*, 1976, *22*, 111–123.

Parke, R. D. Parent-infant interaction: Progress, paradigms, and problems. In G. P. Sackett & H. C. Haywood (Eds.), *Application of observational-ethological methods to the study of mental retardation*. Baltimore: University Park Press, 1978.

Parke, R. D. Interactional designs. In R. B. Cairns (Ed.), *The analysis of social interaction: Methods, issues and illustrations*. Hillsdale, N.J.: Erlbaum, 1979. (a)

Parke, R. D. Perspectives on father-infant interactions. In J. Osofsky (Ed.), *Handbook of infant development*. New York: Wiley, 1979. (b)

Parke, R. D., & O'Leary, S. Father-mother-infant interaction in the newborn period: Some findings, some observations, and some unresolved issues. In M. K. Riegel & J. Meacham (Eds.), *The developing individual in a changing world* (Vol. II). *Social and environment issues*. The Hague: Mouton, 1976.

Parke, R. D., O'Leary, S. E., & West, S. Mother-father-newborn interaction: Effects of maternal medication, labor and sex of infant. *Proceedings of the American Psychological Association*, 1972, 85–86.

Parke, R. D., Power, T. G., & Gottman, J. Conceptualizing and quantifying influence patterns in the family triad. In M. E. Lamb, S. J. Suomi, & G. R. Stephenson (Eds.), *Social interactional analysis: Methodological issues*. Madison: University of Wisconsin Press, 1979.

Parke, R. D., & Sawin, D. B. Infant characteristics and behavior as elicitors of maternal and paternal responsivity in the newborn period. Paper presented at a symposium, "Direction of Effects in Studies of Early Parent-Infant Interaction," at *Society for Research in Child Development*, Denver, April 1975.

Parke, R. D., & Sawin, D. B. The father's role in infancy: A re-evaluation. *The Family Coordinator*, 1976, *25*, 365–371.

Parke, R. D., & Sawin, D. B. Father-infant interaction in the newborn period: A re-evaluation of some current myths. In E. M. Hetherington and R. D. Parke (Eds.), *Contemporary readings in child psychology*. New York: McGraw-Hill, 1977.

Parsons, T., & Bales, R. F. *Family, socialization, and interaction process*. Glencoe, Ill.: Free Press, 1955.

Pedersen, F. Mother, father and infant as an interactive system. Paper presented at the annual convention of the American Psychological Association, Chicago, 1975.

Pedersen, F. A. Does research on children reared in father-absent families yield information on father influence? *The Family Coordinator*, 1976, *25*, 459–464.

Pedersen, F. A., & Robson, K. S. Father participation in infancy. *American Journal of Orthopsychiatry*, 1969, *39*, 466–472.

Pedersen, F., Yarrow, L., Anderson, B., & Cain, R. Conceptualization of father influences in the infancy period. In M. Lewis & L. Rosenblum (Eds.), *The social network of the developing infant*. New York: Plenum, 1979.

Price, G. Factors influencing reciprocity in early mother-infant interaction. Paper presented to the Society for Research in Child Development, New Orleans, 1977.

Radin, N. Observed paternal behaviors as antecedents of intellectual functioning in young boys. *Developmental Psychology*, 1973, *8*, 369–376.

Radin, N. The role of the father in cognitive, academic, and intellectual development. In M. E. Lamb (Ed.), *The role of the father in child development*. New York: Wiley, 1976.

Rapoport, R. Sex-role stereotyping in studies of marriage and the family. In J. Chetrynd & O. Harnett (Eds.), *The sex role system*. Boston: Routledge & Kegan Paul, 1978.

Rebelsky, F., & Hanks, C. Fathers' verbal interaction with infants in the first three months of life. *Child Development*, 1971, *42*, 63–68.

Redican, W. K. Adult male-infant interactions in nonhuman primates. In M. E. Lamb (Ed.), *The role of the father in child development*. New York: Wiley, 1976.

Rendina, I., & Dickerscheid, J. D. Father involvement with firstborn infants. *The Family Coordinator*, 1976, *25*, 373–379.

Richards, M. P. M., Dunn, J. F., & Antonis, B. Caretaking in the first year of life: The role of fathers' and mothers' social isolation. Unpublished manuscript, University of Cambridge, 1975.

Rollins, B. C., & Galligan, R. The developing child and marital satisfaction of parents. In R. M. Lerner & G. B. Spanier (Eds.), *Child influences on marital and family interaction*. New York: Academic Press, 1978.

Rosenblatt, J. S. The development of maternal responsiveness in the rat. *American Journal of Orthopsychiatry*, 1969, *39*, 36–56.

Rosenthal, R. *Experimenter effects in behavioral research*. New York: Appleton-Century-Crofts, 1966.

Ross, G., Kagan, J., Zelazo, P., & Kotelchuck, M. Separation protest in infants in home and laboratory. *Developmental Psychology*, 1975, *11*, 256–257.

Rozelle, R. M., & Campbell, D. T. More plausible rival hypotheses in the cross-lagged panel correlation technique. *Psychological Bulletin*, 1969, *71*, 74–80.

Rubin, J. Z., Provenzano, F. J., & Luria, Z. The eye of the beholder: Parents' views on sex of newborns. *American Journal of Orthopsychiatry*, 1974, *43*, 720–731.

Russell, C. Transition to parenthood: Problems and gratification. *Journal of Marriage and the Family*, 1974, *36*, 294–301.

Russell, G. The father role and its relation to masculinity, femininity, and androgyny. *Child Development*, 1978, *49*, 1174–1181.

Sawin, D. B., Langlois, J., & Leitner, E. F. What do you do after you say hello? Observing, coding, and analyzing parent-infant interactions. *Behavior Research Methods and Instrumentation*, 1977, *9*, 425–428.

Sawin, D. B., & Parke, R. D. Father-infant interaction: Assessment and current status. Paper presented at the Texas Psychological Association Annual Meeting, San Antonio, December 1975.

Sawin, D. B., & Parke, R. D. Adolescent fathers: Some implications from recent research on paternal roles. *Educational Horizons*, 1976, *55*, 38–43.

Schaffer, H. R., & Emerson, P. E. The development of social attachments in infancy. *Monographs of the Society for Research in Child Development*, 1964, *29* (3, Whole No. 94).

Schaffer, R. *Mothering*. Cambridge: Harvard University Press, 1977.

Sears, R. R., Maccoby, E. E., & Levin, H. *Patterns of child rearing*. Evanston, Ill.: Row Peterson, 1957.

Smith, C., & Lloyd, B. Maternal behavior and perceived sex of infant: Revisited. *Child Development*, 1978, *49*, 1263–1265.

Smith, P. K., & Daglish, L. Sex differences in parent and infant behavior in the home. *Child Development*, 1977, *48*, 1250–1254.

Spelke, E., Zelazo, P., Kagan, J., & Kotelchuck, M. Father interaction and separation protest. *Developmental Psychology*, 1973, *9*, 83–90.

Spence, J. T., & Helmreich, R. L. *Masculinity and femininity*. Austin: University of Texas Press, 1978.

Spiker, D. An observational study of problem solving behavior in six preschoolers. Paper presented at the biennial meeting of the Society for Research in Child Development, New Orleans, 1977.

Stoltz, L. M. *Father relations of war-born children*. Stanford: Stanford University Press, 1954.

Suomi, S. J. Adult male-infant interactions among monkeys living in nuclear families. *Child Development*, 1977, *48*, 1255–1270.

Switzky, L. T., Vietze, P., & Switzky, H. Attitudinal and demographic predictors of breast-feeding and bottle-feeding behavior in mothers of six-week-old infants. *Psychological Reports*, 1979, *45*, 3–14.

Tanzer, C., & Block, J. *Why natural childbirth?* New York: Doubleday, 1972.

Tasch, R. J. Interpersonal perceptions of fathers and mothers. *Journal of Genetic Psychology*, 1955, *87*, 59–65.

Tracy, R. L., Lamb, M. E., & Ainsworth, M. D. S. Infant approach behavior as related to attachment. *Child Development*, 1976, *47*, 571–578.

Tulkin, S. R., & Cohler, B. J. Child-rearing attitudes and mother-child interaction in the first year of life. *Merrill-Palmer Quarterly*, 1973, *19*, 95–106.

Tunnell, G. B. Three dimensions of naturalness: An expanded definition of field research. *Psychological Bulletin*, 1977, *84*, 426–437.

U. S. Department of Labor. *Working mothers and their children*. Washington, D. C.: U. S. Government Printing Office, 1977.

Wachs, T. Utilization of a Piagetian approach in the investigation of early experience effects: A research strategy and some illustrative data. *Merrill-Palmer Quarterly*, 1976, *22*, 11–30.

Walker, K. Time use for care of family members. Use-of-Time Research Project, Human Ecology, Cornell University, Working Paper No. 1, September 1972.

Waters, E. The reliability and stability of individual differences in infant-mother attachment. *Child Development*, 1978, *49*, 484–494.

Watson, J. Smiling, cooing and "the game." *Merrill-Palmer Quarterly*, 1972, *18*, 323–339.

Webb, E., Campbell, D., Schwartz, R., & Secrest, L. *Unobtrusive measures*. Chicago: Rand McNally, 1966.

Weinraub, M., & Frankel, J. Sex differences in parent-infant interaction during free play, departure, and separation. *Child Development*, 1977, *48*, 1240–1249.

Weinraub, M., & Lewis, M. The determinants of children's response to separation. *Monographs of the Society for Research in Child Development*, 1977, *42* (4, Serial No. 172).

Weissler, A., & McCall, A. Exploration and play: Resumé and redirections. *American Psychologist*, 1976, *31*, 492–508.

Weist, R. M., & Kruppe, B. Parent and sibling comprehension of children's speech. *Journal of Psycholinguistic Research*, 1977, *6*, 49–58.

Wente, A. S., & Crockenberg, S. B. Transition to fatherhood: Lamaze preparation, adjustment difficulty and the husband-wife relationship. *The Family Coordinator*, 1976, *25*, 351–357.

West, M. M., & Konner, M. J. The role of the father: An anthropological perspective. In M. E. Lamb (Ed.), *The role of the father in child development*. New York: Wiley, 1976.

White, R. W. Motivation reconsidered: The concept of competence. *Psychological Review*, 1959, *66*, 297–333.

Will, J., Self, P., & Datan, N. Maternal behavior and perceived sex of infant. *American Journal of Orthopsychiatry*, 1976, *46*, 135–139.

Willems, E. P. Relations of models to methods in behavioral ecology. In H. McGurk (Ed.), *Ecological factors in human development*. Amsterdam: North-Holland, 1977.

Willemsen, E., Flaherty, D., Heaton, C., & Ritchey, G. Attachment behavior of one-year-olds as a function of mother vs. father, sex of child, session, and toys. *Genetic Psychology Monographs*, 1974, *90*, 305–325.

Wills, T. A., Weiss, R. L., & Patterson, G. R. A behavioral analysis of the determinants of marital satisfaction. *Journal of Consulting and Clinical Psychology*, 1974, *42*, 802–811.

Winthrop, H. Cultural determinants of psychological research values. *The Journal of Social Psychology*, 1961, *53*, 255–269.

Wyer, R. Effect of child rearing attitudes and behavior on children's responses to hypothetical social situations. *Journal of Personality and Social Psychology*, 1965, *2*, 480–486.

Yang, R. K., & Moss, H. A. Neonatal precursors of infant behavior. *Developmental Psychology*, 1978, *14*, 607–613.

Yarrow, L. J. Attachment and dependency: A developmental perspective. In J. L. Gewirtz (Ed.), *Attachment and dependency*. Washington: Winston, 1972.

Yarrow, L. The origins of mastery motivation. Paper presented at the annual meeting of the American Academy of Child Psychiatry, Toronto, Canada, October 1976.

Yarrow, L., Klein, R., Lomonaco, S., & Morgan, G. Cognitive and motivational development in early childhood. In B. Freidlander, G. Sterritt, & G. Kirk (Eds.), *The exceptional infant* (Vol. 3). *Assessment and intervention*. New York: Bruner/Mazel, 1975.

Yarrow, L., Morgan, G., Jennings, K., Harmon, R., & Gaiter, J. The conceptualization and measurement of mastery motivation. Unpublished manuscript, National Institute of Child Health and Human Development, Bethesda, Maryland, 1978.

Yarrow, L., & Pedersen, F. The interplay between cognition and motivation in infancy. In M. Lewis (Ed.), *Origins of intelligence*. New York: Plenum Press, 1976.

Yarrow, L. J., Rubinstein, J. L., & Pedersen, F. A. *Infant and environment: Early cognitive and motivational development*. New York: Halsted Press, 1975.

Yarrow, M. R., Campbell, J. B., & Burton, R. V. *Child rearing*. San Francisco: Jossey-Bass, 1968.

Yogman, M. The goals and structure of face-to-face interaction between infants and fathers. Paper presented at the meetings of the Society for Research in Child Development, New Orleans, March 1977.

Yogman, M., Dixon, S., Tronick, E., Adamson, L., Als, H., & Brazelton, T. Development of infant social interaction with fathers. Paper presented to the Eastern Psychological Association, New York, 1976.

Young, S. F. Paternal involvement as related to maternal employment and attachment behavior directed to the father by the one-year-old infant. Unpublished doctoral dissertation, Ohio State University, 1975.

Zelazo, P. R., Kotelchuck, M., Barber, L., & David, J. Fathers and sons: An experimental facilitation of attachment behaviors. Paper presented at the meetings of the Society for Research in Child Development, New Orleans, March 1977.

INDEX

Harmon, R., 89
Hartup, W., 47
Hays, W., 147
Heath, D., 159
Heaton, C., 25
Hebb, D., 5
Heilbrun, A., 14, 32
Helmreich, R., 14
Herzog, E., 15, 68
Hess, E., 6
Hetherington, E., 32
Hill, R., 6, 71
Hinde, R., 23, 69
Hoffman, L., 12, 13, 153
Hoffman, M., 88
Hogarty, P., 144
Honzik, M., 88
Hunt, J., 5
husband-wife relationship, 6, 7, 20, 73,
  80-81, 85, 154-55, 158-60

identification, 31-32
indirect effects, 7, 42, 128, 144, (*see also*)
  second-order effects
Ingham, M., 25, 41, 88, 112, 113
Inhelder, B., 89
instrumental role, 3
intervention, 109-10
interview methods, 7, 16-17, 18

Jacklin, C., 67, 68, 141, 142
Jennings, K., 89
Johnson, M., 68

Kagan, J., 17, 89
Kaplan, E., 159
Kearsley, R., 89
Keller, H., 113
Kennell, J., 11
Kessen, W., 109
Kitzinger, S., 10
Klaus, M., 11, 45
Konner, M., 67, 68
Koslowski, B., 88
Kotelchuck, M., 17, 25, 41, 67, 69, 88,
  112, 142, 145, 158
Kruppe, B., 141
!Kung San, 67

laboratory studies, 17-18, 25
Laing, R. D., 160

Lamaze, F., 10
Lamb, M., 23, 24, 25, 26, 31, 34, 35, 40,
  41, 42, 67, 69, 72, 77, 79, 91, 100,
  111, 112, 139, 140, 143, 152-55
Lambie, D., 109
Lansky, L., 68
Larzelere, R., 147
Leiderman, P., 159
Leifer, A., 159
Lerner, R., 87
Levenstein, P., 109
Levin, H., 32, 68
Lewis, M., 7, 24, 46, 88, 89, 101, 112,
  141, 150
Lezine, I., 89
Lind, R., 45
Lloyd, B., 152
Lowe, M., 89
Luria, Z., 67
Lynn, D., 68, 140
Lytton, H., 8, 112, 140, 141

Maccoby, E., 32, 67, 68, 142
Martyna, W., 142
Marvin, R., 153
maternal deprivation, 5-6
maternal employment, 9, 12-13, 48
McCall, R., 89, 95, 96, 142, 144
Mead, M., 150
Mendes, H., 158
Messer, S., 142
methodology, 7-8, 15-19, 25-26, 47-51,
  59, 73-75, 90-96, 113-22, 147-48
Mischel, W., 68
Money, J., 32
Morgan, G., 89
Morris, N., 111
Moss, H., 112, 152, 156

Nakamura, C., 145
Norton, A., 148

Oakley, A., 3, 150, 159
observational methods, 7, 17-18, 74-75,
  90-94, 114-18
observer influences, 17-18, 25-26, 91
oedipal period, 34
Olsen, D., 7
Orlansky, H., 5
Orne, M., 18
Orthner, 14

Weiss, R., 74
Weissler, A., 89
Weist, R., 141
West, M., 66, 67, 68, 77, 151
White, R., 5
Will, J., 152
Willems, E., 18
Willemsen, E., 25, 88
Wills, T., 74
Winthrop, H., 2

Wood, D., 141
Wyer, R., 88

Yang, R., 156
Yarrow, L., 23, 74, 89, 99, 100
Yarrow, M., 8
Yogman, M., 72, 88, 112, 139
Young, S., 12

Zelazo, P., 17, 25, 89, 109, 145

ABOUT THE AUTHORS

BARBARA J. ANDERSON obtained her graduate degree from Peabody College. Following an appointment with the National Institute of Child Health and Human Development, she is currently with the St. Louis Children's Hospital, Washington University School of Medicine, St. Louis, Missouri.

JAY BELSKY received his graduate degree from Cornell University. He is now Assistant Professor of Human Development, Division of Individual and Family Studies, College of Human Development, Pennsylvania State University.

RICHARD L. CAIN, JR. pursued his graduate training at the University of Maryland and is now with the National Institute of Child Health and Human Development, Bethesda, Maryland.

K. ALISON CLARKE-STEWART received her graduate degree in developmental psychology from Yale University. She is Associate Professor in the Departments of Education and Behavioral Sciences at the University of Chicago.

MICHAEL LAMB received his graduate education at Yale University. After an appointment at the University of Wisconsin, he is currently with the Psychology Department and Center for Human Growth and Development, University of Michigan, Ann Arbor, Michigan.

ROSS D. PARKE received his Ph.D. degree from Waterloo University and is Professor and Chairman, Division of Developmental Psychology, Department of Psychology, University of Illinois, Champaign, Illinois.

· DOUGLAS B. SAWIN received his graduate education at the University of Minnesota. He is now Assistant Professor of Psychology, University of Texas, Austin, Texas.

FRANK A. PEDERSEN received his Ph.D. degree from Ohio State University. He is currently Chief, Section on Parent-Child Interaction in the Child and Family Research Branch, National Institute of Child Health and Human Development, Bethesda, Maryland.